THE
Complete
Library Trustee
Handbook

Sally Gardner Reed

Jillian Kalonick

For the Association of Library Trustees,
Advocates, Friends and Foundations

Neal-Schuman Publishers, Inc.

New York   London

Published by Neal-Schuman Publishers, Inc.
100 William St., Suite 2004
New York, NY 10038

Printed and bound in the United States of America.

The paper used in this publication meets the minimum requirements of American National Standard for Information Sciences—Permanence of Paper for Printed Library Materials, ANSI Z39.48-1992.

Library of Congress Cataloging-in-Publication Data

Reed, Sally Gardner, 1953-
    The complete library trustee handbook / Sally Gardner Reed and Jillian Kalonick for the Association of Library Trustees, Advocates, Friends and Foundations (ALTAFF).
        p. cm.
    Includes bibliographical references and index.
    ISBN 978-1-55570-687-6 (alk. paper)
    1. Library trustees—United States—Handbooks, manuals, etc. 2. Public libraries—United States—Administration—Handbooks, manuals, etc. I. Kalonick, Jillian. II. Association of Library Trustees, Advocates, Friends and Foundations. III. Title.

Z681.7.U5R445 2010
021.8'2—dc22
                                                                        2010000232

Contents

List of Figures

Preface

The most important job for a board of trustees is to ensure that the library has the resources it needs and is well positioned to deliver excellent services to the community. This means that the budget is sound and sufficient; the library director is an excellent manager of the library and is a leader in the community; the board and library staff regularly engage in strategic planning to ensure that its collections and services are meeting the needs of the community in changing times; and the library has established a set of policies that governs and guides service delivery and personnel in a way that is equitable, fair, and respects the rights of all library users and staff.

It is the unusual trustee who takes on this role with full understanding of the responsibilities involved and an understanding of exactly how a library is governed and managed. This book is designed to guide both new and seasoned trustees through the full scope of trustee responsibilities and will help both to continually improve and evaluate the quality of their governance. Though not all boards are created equal—some are governing boards with full authority over the library while others are advisory, the final authority for the library residing with the city's or county's manager or mayor—this book is designed to help both achieve excellence.

Divided into seven chapters, *The Complete Library Trustee Handbook* will take you through the philosophical and legal foundations for your role, ways to get the funding the library needs, how to work effectively with the director, how to understand and design policy, and how to conduct board business effectively, as well as how to evaluate that effectiveness. We've culled through hundreds of sample policies and documents to share with you the very best so you can see how well your own policies and governing documents match up. If you are creating new documents, the many examples included will serve as excellent guides.

Chapter 1 begins with the extremely important role the library plays in the community and the attendant importance of the role of trustee. With guidance for understanding your fiduciary responsibility, the chapter also includes sample conflict of interest and ethics statements, a template for developing board bylaws, and an example of bylaws that fit neatly into the recommendations of the template.

Finally, Chapter 1 discusses the necessary protections for board members in the execution of their duties.

Chapter 2 looks at the important role that the library's budget and other financial resources play in a library's successfully meeting its mission. Ensuring excellent (at best) or adequate (at least) resources is an important function for trustees. The chapter includes a fairly detailed plan for raising the profile of the library in the community through public awareness that is geared toward helping those who fund you understand the value of the library and its high return on investment. There is also a solid outline for implementing an advocacy campaign when the funding just isn't there. Finally, there is advice on making effective budget presentations, and a blueprint for engaging in a capital campaign.

Chapter 3 addresses the trustee relationship with the most important resource of all—the library director. A library will ever be only as strong as its director. In fact, it could be argued that even the best of budgets won't make up for a director who does not have the respect of his or her staff, who is not recognized and respected in the community, and who does not work constantly to find ways of improving and expanding on existing library services. Because the director is so important, it is critical for trustees to hire the right person, be diligent about evaluating his or her performance, and be willing to dismiss a director who is not measuring up to the board's stated expectations. This chapter will give you what you need to do all of this. In addition, you'll find an overview of the role of the board versus that of the library director in all areas of library management and governance.

Chapter 4 guides you through the strategic planning process—your best tool for helping the library advance and improve in a changing environment. You'll learn all about environmental scanning—how to assess current library effectiveness, how to understand the community's perceptions and expectations, and how to determine what trends at the local, state, and national levels are or will be likely to affect your library. We'll walk you through the vision, mission, and goal-setting processes with examples from other libraries. You will learn about your role in both these areas as well as in evaluating and monitoring the plan's effectiveness.

Chapter 5 delves into the world of library policies. Policies govern the decisions made by staff members on a daily basis. They represent your voice in ensuring that services are delivered in an equitable manner while maximizing the use of library resources for everyone. This chapter includes a number of excellent policies from libraries large and small from across the country that will enable you to benchmark your own. Sample policies in this chapter represent some of the most important in today's world such as Internet use, collection development, acceptable conduct in the library, meeting room use, and more.

Chapter 6 guides you in the actual practical work of being an excellent trustee. Included is a discussion on how and why your board should have a good new trustee orientation process. There is advice on how to hold highly effective board meetings, what to expect from the director in advance of meetings so that you can make good and well-informed decisions, and the board's role versus that of the director in the meeting, as well as a comprehensive guide on board self-evaluation. The more the board can work effectively, the more they can make valuable contributions to the library they serve.

Chapter 7 provides an overview of the issues that potentially affect all public libraries. Issues such as pay equity and privacy are fundamental to your library and a wise trustee will be knowledgeable about them and understand their impact on quality services. Many of these issues are already or will be addressed in library policy; others, such as the privatization of publicly funded libraries, might be news to you. Whether protecting intellectual freedom or the citizens' right to preserve the nonprofit status of its library, understanding the issue and what's at stake is critical to good governance.

Two appendixes complete this handbook. The first is "A Selected List of Best Sources for Further Reading and Learning"—the very best sources of information for trustees. The second is "Essential Documents Every Trustee Needs," a comprehensive compendium of policy statements from the American Library Association that inform the practice of libraries across the country. These policy statements will, no doubt, be invaluable as foundation documents for governance.

The Association of Library Trustees, Advocates, Friends and Foundations designed *The Complete Library Trustee Handbook* to demystify library governance for you and provide you with all you will need to know to be a great board member. As part of a board, you will find out what it takes collectively to work as a first-rate team, taking the library to ever greater heights and ensuring that the library is so visible and well respected in the community that it gets all the support it needs to deliver the very best in library services, has a top-notch director, follows excellent policies and practices, and always keeps an eye to the future.

1

Library Trustees: Guardians of the Public Trust

Being a library trustee is a noble undertaking for one of America's most venerable institutions—the public library. Perhaps the most important job of the library trustee is to understand how significant this position is. Trustees must honor the library with full commitment to govern well, to be engaged within the community to promote the library, and to learn all they can about the important and unique role that the library plays in the community.

It is impossible to imagine our democracy without well-educated and informed citizens. And while there are certainly many avenues to information—the media, newspapers and magazines, the Internet—there is only one place where one can climb into history and into the minds of some of the world's greatest thinkers over the ages; where one can discover a new idea and follow it endlessly through stacks of books and screens on terminals; where children can embrace the joy of reading and listening and chase down any path their minds and imaginations take them; where anyone can find solace, comfort, humor, and understanding by reading the works of others. It's the library.

The library's commitment to provide every individual the resources he or she is looking for is an important component of what makes for an educated citizen. It's not what is fed to us in sound bites over the Internet and on television. It's not even our formal education. It's our lifelong education—our search, as individuals, to find meaning in the world around us from the first day we toddle into a library until that last batch of library books is delivered by outreach services. Library patrons are natural seekers. Whether it's biography, philosophy, how-to-do-it guidance, fiction, or finance, our patrons want to learn and understand.

Libraries foster and support the well-informed, self-governing individuals upon which our democracy depends. In this way, and in many others, even those who don't use the library benefit. The entire society benefits when there is a well-educated populace that has free and unfettered access to a library's resources so they can be active and productive citizens. The entire society benefits when job seekers come into the library to search for jobs online and get support on résumé writing and interview skills, thereby becoming employed and tax-paying citizens. The entire society benefits when children learn a love of books well before entering kindergarten, thereby greatly enhancing their chances of completing school successfully and becoming tomorrow's productive and engaged citizens.

Perhaps no one has better summarized the power and the beauty of the library than Toni Morrison:

> Access to knowledge is the superb, the supreme act of truly great civilizations. Of all the institutions that purport to do this, free libraries stand virtually alone in accomplishing this mission. No committee decides who may enter, no crisis of body or spirit must accompany the entrant. No tuition is charged, no oath sworn, no visa demanded. Of the monuments humans build for themselves, very few say "touch me, use me, my hush is not indifference, my space is not barrier. If I inspire awe, it is because I am in awe of you and the possibilities that dwell in you."[1]

This is the treasure you have under your watch. Your job is to protect this institution and uphold its mission. You must uphold the public's trust in you to ensure that the library is well run, meets the needs of the members of your community, responds to a changing environment, and safeguards the right of every citizen in your community to receive equitable and unfettered access to excellent library services and collections.

Governing versus Advisory Boards

Generally speaking, there are two types of boards of trustees—governing and advisory. A governing board is one that has the final authority and responsibility for the library and its services. Governing board members are generally elected to their positions or appointed by elected officials. The governing board has legal and fiduciary responsibilities, hires and fires the library director, sets policy, determines the library mission, and is directly accountable to the public.

If the library is a city or county department, it is very likely that the board will be an advisory board because the director will be hired and fired by the city manager or mayor and will be directly accountable to him or her as a department head. An advisory board is typically appointed by the governing authorities of the community service area and has the responsibility to give input into the library's planning process, policy setting, and promotional plans, and may even participate in the hiring and evaluation of the director. This board does not have the same legal and fiduciary responsibilities as a governing board, but the members are still representatives of the public and can be incredibly important volunteers and advocates for the library.

Both boards, however, do have responsibilities in common. Both should know and understand the local ordinances and state laws that impact the library and its operations. Both boards should be familiar with the library's budget, what the funding mix for the library is, and from where the funding is derived. Both boards should promote the library's budget to the funding authorities. Both boards should be involved in the planning process and both should have input into the setting of library policy. Perhaps most importantly, both boards should be strong library advocates.

Fiduciary Responsibility for Governing Boards

Governing boards have both legal and fiduciary responsibilities. Many trustees take this to mean that they are responsible for ensuring that the library's budget is spent well and fully in accordance with the library's mission, and that the library operates within the law. Certainly, these are important aspects of their duties.

Fiduciary responsibility, however, should be viewed in much broader terms—especially in relationship to an entity as important as the public library. Stephen R. Smith, in writing about the duties of a nonprofit board, says that fiduciary responsibilities extend to duty of due care, duty of obedience, and duty of loyalty. Duty of care, he says, "requires that a director [trustee] perform his or her responsibilities as a board member in good faith and with the care that an ordinarily prudent person in a like position would use under similar circumstances." In addition, he lists the following as requirements for acting with due care and due obedience:

- Adopting policies and procedures that provide for effective oversight of management
- Attending board and committee meetings to which they are assigned so that they will have an opportunity to obtain the information necessary to make an informed judgment about matters on which they must make decisions on behalf of the corporation [library]
- Acting in an independent manner and exercising independent judgment in matters affecting the nonprofit
- Ensuring that the nonprofit acts in accordance with its exempt purposes[2]

The duty of loyalty is basically one that requires that individual trustees always act in the best interest of the library and never in their own best interest. Because of the importance of this obligation, it is wise for boards to require that every member sign conflict of interest and ethics statements. If your board does not already have these in place, working on their development will give everyone an opportunity to reflect on their positions as well as safeguard against any future actions of malfeasance by members. Figures 1.1 and 1.2 show examples.

Figure 1.1. Sample Conflict of Interest Policy

Anytown Public Library
Conflict of Interest Policy
Officers, Board Members, and Employees

No board member or committee member of the Anytown Public Library shall derive any personal profit or gain, directly or indirectly, by reason of his or her participation on the board. Other than compensation, no employee shall derive any personal profit or gain, directly or indirectly, by reason of his or her employment by the Anytown Public Library except through activities that may facilitate professional advancement or contribute to the profession such as publications and professional service and have been fully disclosed to the board.

Each individual shall disclose to the board any personal interest which he or she may have in any matter pending before the board and shall refrain from participation in any decision on such matter.

Members of Anytown Public Library Board, committees, and staff shall refrain from obtaining any list of library patrons that results in personal benefit.

Statement of Associations

This is to certify that I, except as described on the reverse of this sheet, am not now nor at any time during the past year have been:

> A participant, directly or indirectly, in any arrangement, agreement, investment, or other activity with any vendor, supplier, or other party doing business with Anytown Public Library that has resulted or could result in personal benefit to me.

Any exceptions to the above are stated on the reverse of this sheet with a full description of the transactions, whether direct or indirect, which I have (or have had during the past year) with persons or organizations having transactions with Anytown Public Library.

Signature: _____ Date: _____

Printed name: _____

Anytown Public Library position: _____

Directors and Officers Insurance

The subject of trustee liability is one that should be taken seriously and addressed. Federal and state laws in many cases protect individuals from harm in a lawsuit if they have acted in good faith—even if a decision they made turned out to be one of poor judgment or erroneous. In addition, anyone bringing suit against an individual trustee or trustees has the burden of proof to show that the individuals did not act in good faith.

That's all well and good, but protecting trustees from liability when acting in accordance with their fiduciary responsibilities won't necessarily keep someone from trying. The cost to any individual board member to defend against a lawsuit can be very significant. Therefore, it behooves the board as a whole to indemnify members in the case of lawsuits. Indemnification means that the board will cover any costs for defense of a member or members if in the end there is no judgment against them.

Figure 1.2. Sample Ethics Policy

Anytown Public Library
Ethics Policy

The Anytown Public Library is dependent on the trust of its community to successfully achieve its mission. Therefore, it is crucial that all board members and employees conduct business on behalf of the Anytown Public Library with the highest level of integrity, avoiding any impropriety or the appearance of impropriety.

Guiding Principles:

- Board members and employees should uphold the integrity of the Anytown Public Library and should perform their duties impartially and diligently.
- Board members and employees should not engage in discrimination of any kind including that based on race, class, ethnicity, religion, sex, sexual orientation, or belief system.
- Board members and employees should protect and uphold library patrons' right to privacy in their use of the library's resources.
- Board members and employees should avoid situations in which their personal interests, activities, or financial affairs are, or are likely to be perceived as being in conflict with the best interests of the Anytown Public Library.
- Board members and employees should avoid having interests that may reasonably bring into question their position in a fair, impartial and objective manner.
- Board members and employees should not knowingly act in any way that would reasonably be expected to create an impression among the public that they are engaged in conduct that violates their trust as board members or employees.
- Board members and employees should not use or attempt to use their position with the Anytown Public Library to obtain unwarranted privileges or advantages for themselves or others.
- Board members and employees should not be swayed by partisan interests, public pressure, or fear of criticism.
- Board members and employees should not denigrate the organization or fellow board members or employees in any public arena.

Therefore:

To preserve and uphold the Anytown Public Library's reputation as an organization of unimpeachable integrity, each board member and employee will sign a conflict of interest statement and an ethics statement at the beginning of each calendar year (and at the commencement of their service) during their tenure with the Anytown Public Library.

Compliance:

If any board member or the executive director appears to be in conflict with the Guiding Principles above, he or she will be asked to meet with the executive committee to discuss the issue. The executive committee will make a recommendation to the full board based on their findings. Employees who are or appear to be in conflict with the Guiding Principles will be asked to meet with the executive director, who will make a determination as to discipline or termination based on his or her findings.

Signature: _____ Date: _____

Printed name: _____

Anytown Public Library position: _____

The board can protect itself from legal defense costs by having directors and officers (D&O) insurance. Coverage by this insurance can be extended to individual trustees or can cover the board itself in the case where it indemnifies its trustees for reimbursement of expenses.

Some boards may well be covered by their parent organization if part of a larger government body such as the county or city. It's a good idea to find out. If the board does not have this protection, they should look into and carefully compare D&O policies. According to Smith, the following are important steps to take:

- The nonprofit's management should retain the services of a knowledgeable insurance broker who can ensure that the proper coverage is provided at the most affordable rate.

- Directors should review the coverage and terms with management and should ask questions regarding the proposed policy.

- The company chosen to provide the coverage should be highly rated by the insurance rating agencies.

- The policy should require the insurance company to provide the corporation and its directors with a defense against any lawsuit and to pay for that defense.

- Careful attention should be paid to the notice provisions of the policy since the failure to comply with required notice to the insurance company of a potential or pending lawsuit may, in some instances, invalidate the coverage.[3]

Note that many confuse D&O with errors and omissions (E&O) insurance, but they are not the same. D&O insurance is concerned with the performance and duties of management and governance. E&O is concerned with performance failures and negligence with respect to your products and services. It is a good idea to have both if at all possible, but if you only are able to get one kind of coverage, the best for boards and board members is the D&O insurance.

Bylaws

It's important for all boards of trustees to have bylaws. This set of rules will govern how the board operates and ensure that all members of the board clearly understand their role. Bylaws ensure consistency and objectivity in carrying out the board's activities. In addition, the bylaws will serve as additional protection for the board if it is ever sued when the board and its members have been acting within the bylaw's prescripts. Whether a governing or advisory board, bylaws are often required by state library associations to meet standards.

Many state libraries will have guidelines and assistance for the development of bylaws. The following comes from Michigan's Department of History, Arts, and Libraries:

1. Legal authority: This provision should give the full legal name of the library and make reference to the establishment statute or the source of the library's existence; e.g., the County Libraries Act or the city charter.

2. Library Board: The number of board members, whether the members are elected or appointed, the length of a member's term, the date on which the members' terms begin, and the powers and duties of the board members should all be stated. If there is statutory authority for the powers and duties, or if they are delegated powers, that reference should be included.

3. Officers: The officers should be listed, as well as the method of selecting officers and the duties and powers of each.

4. Board meetings: Several items should be included in this provision, such as regular meeting dates, meeting place, posting of notices, and the usual "Order of Business." Compliance with the Michigan Open Meetings Act should be specifically stated. The "Order of Business" gives both trustees and the public a structure to rely on for the orderly progress of the board meetings. Many boards provide the recording secretary with a template of the "Order of Business" as an aid for taking minutes. A typical "Order of Business" may include the following items:
   a. Call to order
   b. Approval of the agenda
   c. Approval of the last meeting's minutes
   d. Treasurer's report
   e. Committee reports
   f. Director's report
   g. Old business
   h. New business
   i. Public comment
   j. Adjournment
   It should be noted that the Open Meetings Act requires an opportunity for public comment. It may be placed on the agenda at whatever part of the meeting the Board deems most helpful.

5. Committees: Provision should be made for standing committees and for the appointment of additional committees as needed.

6. Amending the bylaws: Most boards require a two-thirds vote to amend the bylaws, in contrast to the simple majority required for most other matters.

7. Other provisions: The board may include any other provisions necessary for the proper functioning of the board. Although it is tempting to clutter bylaws with extraneous provisions, this practice should be resisted so that the bylaws address only necessary items.[4]

The Ames Public Library in Iowa has a good set of bylaws that exemplify these criteria (see Figure 1.3).

Figure 1.3. Board of Trustees Bylaws, Ames Public Library (Ames, IA)

Ames Public Library Policy Board of Trustees
Section: Administration Approved: 3/97
Subject: Bylaws, Board of Trustees Reviewed: 3/04, 4/05, 4/06
Revised 3/04, 4/05, 4/06

Following are the bylaws of the Ames Public Library Board of Trustees:

Library Board

1. In accordance with Ordinance No. 784 of the City of Ames, the Ames Public Library Board of Trustees will have nine (9) members. The members are appointed by the Mayor, with the approval of the City Council, and the term of office for each trustee shall be for a six (6) year period with no reappointment. Trustees shall receive no compensation but will be reimbursed for necessary expenses related to their service as trustees.

2. The general powers and duties of the Ames Public Library Board of Trustees are specified in Chapter 15 of the Municipal Code of the City of Ames.

3. The Board will exercise its powers and duties as follows:
   a. Employ a competent and qualified librarian to serve as Director.
   b. Evaluate the performance and effectiveness of the Director in fulfilling his/her duties and responsibilities as prescribed in the Bylaws. This evaluation will be performed annually by the Director Evaluation Committee of the Board and will be discussed with the Director at a March meeting of the Board.
   c. Determine and adopt written policies to govern all operations and programs of the library, in consultation with the Director as necessary.
   d. Report to and cooperate with other public officials, boards and the Ames community in support of a good public relations program within the community.
   e. Prepare and seek adequate support for the annual Library budget.
   f. Develop long-range goals for the Library and work toward the achievement of these goals.
   g. Accept gifts and approve all library expenditures.
   h. Authorize the use of the library by nonresidents of the city.

4. No member of the Board of Trustees shall be financially interested, directly or indirectly, in any contract, sale or transaction that comes before the Board of Trustees for approval or other official action that pertains to the Library.

Officers

1. The officers of the Board will be President, Vice President and Secretary, who shall serve terms of one year, and shall be designated the "Executive Committee." Officers may succeed themselves in office, but may serve no more than three terms in the same office. An officer must be a Board member during his/her term in office.

2. At the February meeting of the Board, the President will appoint a Nominating Committee consisting of two (2) Board members to prepare a slate of candidates for office. This slate, chosen from the current Board members, will be presented to the Board at the April meeting. Nominations for office may then be offered from the floor, after which the Board will vote. Officers will be installed immediately after the election, and will hold office until their successors are elected and installed.

(Continued)

Figure 1.3. Board of Trustees Bylaws, Ames Public Library (Ames, IA) *(Continued)*

Ames Public Library Policy Board of Trustees
Section: Administration Approved: 3/97
Subject: Bylaws, Board of Trustees Reviewed: 3/04, 4/05, 4/06
Revised 3/04, 4/05, 4/06

Officers *(Continued)*

3. The duties of the officers are as follows:
   a. The President will:
      i. preside at all meetings of the Board
      ii. appoint all standing and ad hoc committees
      iii. prepare the agenda for Board meetings
      iv. serve as Chair of the Executive Committee
      v. sign the monthly financial statement presented by the Director as an indication of the acceptance of the statement by the Board
      vi. serve as liaison for the library staff
   b. The Vice President will:
      i. perform such functions as may be assigned by the President or the Board
      ii. serve as a member of the Executive Committee
      iii. perform all the functions of the President in his/her absence or disability
   c. The Secretary will:
      i. record and properly file, in permanent form, complete proceedings of each Board meeting (This responsibility may be discharged with the assistance of appropriate library personnel.)
      ii. send a copy of such proceedings to each Board member prior to the subsequent meeting (This responsibility may be discharged with the assistance of appropriate library personnel.)
      iii. sign the monthly financial statement together with the President
      iv. perform all the functions of the President in the simultaneous absence and/or disability of the President and Vice President
      v. serve as a member of the Executive Committee

Meetings

1. Regular meetings will be held monthly, with the date, hour and location being determined by the Board.
2. Special meetings may be held at any time, at the call of either the President or any three (3) members of the Board; however, at least twenty-four (24) hours advance notice of the special meeting must be given to all Trustees.
3. A quorum at any meeting will consist of five (5) or more Trustees.
4. A vote will be decided by a simple majority of the Trustees voting except in the case where other criteria are required by ordinance or statute.
5. An agenda for each regular Board meeting will be made available to the Trustees prior to the meeting, together with necessary discussion materials.
6. The agenda will be made available to the public at least twenty-four (24) hours prior to the meeting, by posting or advertising it in places generally available to the public.

(Continued)

Figure 1.3. Board of Trustees Bylaws, Ames Public Library (Ames, IA) (Continued)

Ames Public Library Policy Board of Trustees
Section: Administration Approved: 3/97
Subject: Bylaws, Board of Trustees Reviewed: 3/04, 4/05, 4/06
Revised 3/04, 4/05, 4/06

Meetings (Continued)

7. The order of business for regular meetings shall include but not be limited to the following items:

    a. Call to Order
    b. Adoption of Agenda
    c. Public Forum
    d. Financial Reports
    e. Administrative Staff Reports
    f. Friends of the Ames Public Library Report
    g. Ames Public Library Foundation Report
    h. Policy Review
    i. Unfinished Business
    j. New Business
    k. Trustee Comments
    l. Adjournment

8. All meetings of the Board are open to anyone who may wish to observe the proceedings in accordance with the Iowa Open Meetings Law, Iowa Code Chapter 21. Non-Board members who wish to address the Board will be given the opportunity in the Public Forum, for which time will always be designated within the agenda.

9. The latest edition of *The Standard Code of Parliamentary Procedure* by Alice Sturgis will govern the parliamentary procedures of the Board.

Committees/Board Liaison Appointments

1. The President may appoint ad hoc committees as needed. Standing committees must be established by a vote of the Board. If a committee member is unable to serve, a replacement will be appointed by the President. In May of each year, the President will appoint:

    a. Two (2) Trustees to serve as an Arts Advisory Committee, to serve in an advisory capacity to the Board, the Director and Library personnel in the acquisition and acceptance of fine art objects for the Library.

    b. Two (2) Trustees to serve as liaison with the Friends of the Ames Public Library Board.

    c. Two (2) Trustees to serve as representatives to the Ames Public Library Foundation Board of Directors.

    d. Two (2) Trustees to serve as a Budget and Finance Committee. With the assistance of the Director, this Committee prepares the annual general fund budget and regularly reviews private funds and makes recommendations regarding their management. Committee members give policy direction regarding service priorities for personnel, materials, and operations expenditures and for budgeted revenues. Committee members review the capital improvement plan projects and the Library's line-item budget request during the preparation process in September/October and recommend a budget request for Board approval in November. The Budget and Finance Committee members attend the Library's budget hearing with the City Council in February.

2. No committee shall have other than advisory power unless, by suitable action of the Board, it is granted specific power to act.

(Continued)

Figure 1.3. Board of Trustees Bylaws, Ames Public Library (Ames, IA) *(Continued)*

Ames Public Library Policy Board of Trustees
Section: Administration Approved: 3/97
Subject: Bylaws, Board of Trustees Reviewed: 3/04, 4/05, 4/06
Revised 3/04, 4/05, 4/06

The Director

1. The Director's duties and responsibilities are detailed in the Director's General Job Duties Policy in the Ames Public Library Policy Manual.

2. The Director is a non-voting, ex-officio member of the Board of Trustees.

Amendments to Bylaws

1. Amendments to these Bylaws may be adopted by a majority vote at any regular meeting of the Board, provided that notice of the proposed amendments has been given to the Trustees at least seven (7) days prior to the meeting.

Notes

1. Toni Morrison, speaking at the New York Public Library, September 1997.
2. Stephen R. Smith, "Directors and Officers on Behalf of the Board," in *The Nonprofit Legal Landscape*, ed. Ober/Kaler (Washington, DC: BoardSource, 2005), 24–32.
3. Ibid.
4. Michigan Department of Education, "Bylaws for Public Library Boards," www.michigan .gov/mde/0,1607,7-140-54504_18668_18689-54440—,00.html.

2

Library Sustainability: Fund-Raising and Advocacy

You may not have become a library trustee to fight budget battles, raise money for capital campaigns, or to support the work of the Friends group or the library's foundation, but they are all components of your critical role to ensure adequate financial support—especially in today's economic climate. Even the best library director and staff can do only so much to stretch a dollar; it is the trustees' job to be sure that there are plenty of dollars to stretch—enough for excellent library collections and services.

If you are lucky, this only means that you touch base with the city or county council (or other funding body) once a year to be sure that your already excellent budget is keeping pace with your changing needs and the cost of living. If you are lucky, you are in a new or newer building that has plenty of space for all its collections and room for all types of use. The roof isn't leaking; the air conditioning works; and the carpet isn't frayed. If you are lucky, you have a terrific Friends group that is raising money on a regular basis to help the library purchase all those extras that are not normally covered by the library's budget and a foundation that is raising large amounts of money for a rainy day fund, for an endowment, or for high-profile programs and library publicity.

If you are like most in the country, however, your budget isn't keeping pace with service needs and the cost of living. In fact, many libraries are facing budget cuts or being closed altogether. You may have outgrown your space or need additional branches for a growing community. Your library or libraries may need significant renovations and repair. You may not have a Friends group or have one that is faltering or aging out and is unable to recruit new, more energetic members. Any or all of these situations are cause for action on the trustees' part. Luckily for you, creating a sustainable financial situation for your library isn't complicated. It takes some time and effort on your part (maybe more than you'd planned on if you thought all you were going to do was warm a seat at the board table) but the good news is, if you're successful, you will all feel like heroes—and you can be successful.

Securing Financial Resources for the Library

If you checked out a book on library trusteeship from more than a couple of decades ago, you probably wouldn't find the word *advocacy* anywhere inside. That's because, in large part, libraries were pretty well funded until somewhere around the end of the twentieth century. When you think about it, it makes a certain amount of sense. Up until the late twentieth century, library services were quite stable. In essence, libraries lent books to patrons. Some libraries grew as their communities did but, basically, other than books and programs, library services were relatively static. Oh sure, they got pretty wild around the 1950s when libraries started showing and even loaning filmstrips. And there were, of course, LP record, then cassettes, then CDs. But, books were, by and large, the business of libraries.

Around 1990, there was a huge shift. Computers and, more specifically, computerized information came into the mainstream. This has changed everything. Libraries are now as much about information as about books. And while books are still the mainstay, no library can fulfill its mission to be the center for lifelong learning in the community without embracing digital technology in all its forms. This means everything from providing Internet access at public computer terminals to providing high-tech (and high-cost) information databases. Library service has become more complex, more diversified, and more expensive.

The advent of information technology has been a true boon to the work that libraries can do to be able to provide the community with all kinds of information and, yes, entertainment in all kinds of formats. Ideally, this would give libraries even more clout and power in the community—raising them to the level of essential services requiring full funding. Alas, this has not generally been the case. Instead, our local leaders—those who hold the purse strings—are too often ignorant about what the library has to offer and why it matters. There is a prevailing sense among these people that libraries have become more dispensable because (a) you can get everything you need on the Internet, and (b) everyone has the Internet.

Wow, what a job trustees have to do to educate community leaders and members, and advocate for library funding. Because of the diversity of information formats and the expertise needed to provide access to it and meaning from it, libraries have become more costly to operate. Not only do we need the stable funding of the past, we need more of it. Libraries are certainly worth it. That's the message trustees must get out—loud and clear.

As "expensive" as library services are in the twenty-first century, they remain less than 1 percent of all American tax dollars. At the local level, libraries rarely receive more than 4 percent of a community's operating budget, and often it's much less than that. Yet they serve the entire community and provide the only source of an infinite array of information, enlightenment, and entertainment, without charge, to everyone without regard to their means. What could be a better use of tax dollars than that?

Education and advocacy—these are very important areas for trustee focus. It is crucial to educate funders about the critical role libraries play in the information age and advocate for full funding of this service. Both education and advocacy can be simple. It just takes a little thought, a plan, and then action. Education or public awareness, for example, should be an ongoing enterprise. If everyone fully understood what the library has to offer and, importantly, the value of those services to the community, then the funding quest would automatically become easier.

Public Awareness—Creating the Message

A public awareness (education) campaign should be targeted at getting the message out about two important points:

- What the library has to offer
- Why these services matter to the entire community

The first part is easy, and most library staffs and trustees do it all the time. It can be, essentially, a laundry list of services. You can probably tick most of those off the top of your head at a moment's notice. It's the second part, "why these services matter," that is most important and the area in which most public awareness or education campaigns fall short. We who love libraries assume everyone knows why libraries are important but, of course, they don't. Even if they know that your library has public access computers, for example, they may assume that they are mostly used by kids playing video games, or as a way for the homeless population to spend their time.

A good public awareness campaign will focus on educating why each and every service matters—and not only to those who are using them. This isn't as hard a task as you might think. In fact, if you can't articulate the value of each of the library's services, you should end that service. If it doesn't matter, why do it? You have enough on your plates without providing meaningless services. Of course, in the end there probably aren't any libraries providing meaningless services.

Think about it. What are the kinds of services the library offers? Following is a typical list:

- Books—all types of books for all ages on all subjects
- Public-access computers and information databases
- Programs for children and adults
- Audiovisual collections including music, movies, and informational videos
- Reference services
- Bookmobile and outreach services to those who are unable to use the library

This is a pretty good list, but you may be able to add more. It's probably a fair bet that most people in the community are aware of most of these services. Some might be surprised that patrons can download audio books from their home or office computer and others might not know that they can access a database such as LexisNexis for free at their library but, by and large, we've done a fairly good job of letting our communities know what we have to offer.

Now is the time to make sure that every funder and every citizen in the community knows why these services matter—whether they use the library or not. So, let's go back through the list. It's possible make a powerful case for each and every one of them. Imagine that you are making the case for the mayor who never uses the library and wants to cut the library's budget in half. Why, if she never uses the library, should she have to pay for it? Remember, this exercise is not designed to make the mayor into a library user. You want to turn her into a library supporter. You want to educate her on the value of the library—to show her why a relatively small investment in the library pays huge dividends to the community at large.

Getting the Message Out

Once you and the library director have created a list of talking points that are powerful and convincing about the library's value to the community, it's time to get that message out there in as many ways as possible. It's not enough to be able to articulate what the library has to offer and why it matters. Trustees should also see their roles as conduits of this message to the public and, importantly, to those who fund the library. While librarians work hard to inform their communities about the library and its services, the trustees' voice will be seen as the official voice of the library and, therefore, it carries a lot of weight and credibility.

Getting the message out is easy, and there are as many avenues for doing so as your imaginations can come up with. If the board is serious about beginning the education or public awareness process, it would be wise to draw up a plan of action. This doesn't have to be a complex blueprint with goals and objectives; instead, a list of areas for action along with an assignment of responsibility and a deadline for achievement will work fine. The following are some examples of simple but powerful strategies, along with sample timelines and assignments.

Letters to the Editor

Without bombarding the newspaper with a lot of letters (that will come later in the advocacy campaign), you can make the point about the value of the library by asking several library-supportive community VIPs along with the president of the board to write a letters—spaced over time—extolling the importance of the library.

Whether crime, real estate values, unemployment, or other community concerns, there is almost always a way to show that the library is part of the solution. In doing so, you are showing everyone—whether they use the library or not—that the library is important to the community, costs little, and has an impact on us all.

Word of Mouth

The marketing world is all abuzz about word-of-mouth marketing. This simple concept is based on a single individual's ability to influence others. If the board works on getting all their supporters (think Friends) to begin a word-of-mouth campaign, the word about libraries could go viral.

To make this word-of-mouth campaign successful, the board should ensure that everyone they enlist for this easy but effective tactic has a list of talking points—you want the message to be consistent and accurate. Go back to the work you did in creating that message. Select some of the best and most powerful statements and include them on the list. Then meet with or e-mail all those you know you can count on to get the message out. Here are just of few of the ways your recruits can do it:

- Social networking sites (Twitter, Facebook, etc.)
- Talking with friends, neighbors, club members, etc.
- E-mails
- Blogs

Speaker's Bureau

It is entirely likely that board members are active in other organizations as well as the library. Perhaps they are members of civic organizations such as the Rotary Club, the Lions, or Kiwanis. As library board members and as members of other organizations, there is little doubt that they are seen as important representatives of the library and of the community. Board members should use their standing to help educate those within their sphere of influence about the value and cost effectiveness of library services.

Rather than a catch-as-catch-can approach, it is much better to do a little groundwork by identifying all the important groups (social, civic, leisure) in the community and finding out who among you and other library supporters could speak on behalf of the library. Receptive groups might include:

- Rotary club
- Community book club
- Lions club
- Kiwanis club
- Gardening club

By making assignments and establishing deadlines, the person responsible for this strategy can mark his or her calendar to follow up and make sure that the job was done. Sometimes nothing is more powerful than a fellow club or group member making a pitch on behalf of something he or she is passionate about.

Radio

You might be surprised at how effective radio public service announcements can be. If you live in a large market, the cost of air time might be significant, but you can always work to get favorable rates for the library. Yes, there still is a requirement that radio stations give some free airtime to public service announcements (PSAs) but if you want time other than, say, 3 a.m. on Sundays, you will probably have to pay for it. If you live in a smaller community with one or two local radio stations, you may well get primetime for free.

If your board decides that this would be an effective strategy for educating the public about the value of the library, talk to your Friends group and see if it is something they would be willing to fund. The next step is to get an expert to write your PSAs. Again, in a small town, a local DJ might well be willing to do it for you. DJs have the editing equipment, sound effects, and professional voice to do it. Give them the talking points and work with them on what they come up with.

In a larger community, you might either have to pay (dearly) for the creation of the PSA, or you could try a local college or university that has a broadcast program or a campus radio station. A student might well find this an attractive project and may even be able to get credit for it. Working with a student and with your list of talking points, you'll no doubt come up with something that sounds professional—even though it's free.

One on One

Sometimes the most powerful way to make your case is to simply spend time with your community leaders on a one-to-one basis. It is a good idea for board members to take time each year, apart from budget time, to make an appointment with every council member to discuss the library and its services. These can be very positive meetings to discuss the ways in which the library is making a difference in the community.

Each trustee can be assigned a council member to visit. Armed with the talking points you've created, trustees can visit with their council member and tell the library's story. Be sure to let council members know how much you appreciate their support of the library. Let them know the huge impact their relatively small investment in the library is making.

Let them know that in tough times library use goes way up, but also let them know what that means in terms of kids getting homework done and preschoolers getting that book-rich environment that studies show is so important. Let them know those numbers represent job seekers who are finding and getting jobs by using library resources.

Ask the library director to put together a folder of information that shows in the most powerful way possible what the library is doing and how its services are making a positive impact on the community. Be sure and leave this information behind.

Taking time to visit with council members will not go unrecognized—your efforts will be appreciated.

The ways to get the library's message out need only be limited by your imagination, and you should include the Friends in case there are some costs involved. Not only can Friends help pay for some of your ideas, but they can be an excellent source of ideas themselves. Even though you are a library lover, it doesn't mean everyone else in the community is. You don't need to turn everyone into a library user, but there is no reason everyone can't be a library supporter. All it takes is education and getting the word out every day in every way.

Budget Presentations

With a strong public awareness campaign behind you, you will, hopefully, find a more receptive funding body (let's say city council) than you might have met with otherwise. It should be the case that everyone on the council has learned much about the cost-effective value of the library, and they are ready to ensure it has the budget it needs. If so, your job will be easy. If the council is still looking to the library to help balance a tight budget, however, you may have to resort to an all-out advocacy campaign (see the section The Advocacy Campaign on p. 20).

Regardless of the inclination of the council, it is important for the board and director to make the most powerful case for the library's budget request possible. This, in addition to getting the budget the library needs, is also another opportunity to educate your most important audience—the people who ultimately decide your funding level.

There are probably as many different approaches to presenting the library's budget as there are libraries. The most important thing is that you relate your budget to the outcomes that bring value to the community. It is imperative that those who hold your financial future in their hands understand that the library has a high and important impact on your community, and that the cost of providing its services is extremely low—even if they give you all that you are requesting in your budget.

If you have worked on an excellent public awareness campaign, you already have done much of the work to provide a powerful case for your budget request. Working very closely with the director (who is, after all, the single person who knows best what the implications of funding each line are—or what the consequences of not funding each line are), you can take the talking points about the value of each of the library's areas of service and show how the funding you request will maximize that value.

It is entirely possible that the city or town council has a prescribed method of presentation. For example, they may request a written report; they may request a written report in a particular format; they may ask for a PowerPoint presentation; or they may simply ask you to come before them and give an oral defense of your budget request. Regardless of the manner of delivery, you should ensure that you can defend the value of each of the library's programs of service and show how its impact on the community is cost effective.

Do not whine. Yes, the library has probably been historically underfunded. It might well be true that the library is taking a disproportionate percentage of cuts. You may have buildings that are falling apart. While all of this may be true and you should make these issues well known, sounding like a victim has never been a position of strength.

Whatever format you use to present and defend your budget, be positive. Recognize the difficulties the council has in balancing the community's budget. Let them know that you are here to offer them an opportunity to provide solutions to the community's ills. The library creates readers. It helps the unemployed find jobs and therefore pay taxes. It gives teens a fun place to be after school and in the summer and helps keep them off the streets. The library is a community center and is being used now more than ever. It's the best taxpayer bang for the buck going.

As you present your case and your statistics, be sure that there are stories to go along with them. It's not enough to tell how many people visited your library last year; tell them why that number matters. Tell them about Bob J. who used your terminals to find job listings, create a résumé, and respond online to those listings. Let them know that Bob J. came back to thank a librarian when he found a job. Remind the council that hundreds of "Bobs" are included in the number of those who visited the library.

As you talk about the number of books checked out, tell about how reading remains the biggest factor for success. Tell them about Mrs. Z, who moved to your community from Pakistan and didn't speak English. Tell how she was determined that her children would enter the local school with some background in English, and so she visited the children's department, where the youth services librarian helped her pick out high-interest easy readers and connected her with a community tutor for the children. Let them know that this has reduced the remediation necessary to bring them up to grade when they entered school, thus saving the taxpayers money.

Your statistics matter, but the impact and stories behind those numbers matter more. Work with the director to isolate some of those stories (they are happening in the library every day) and put together a presentation that tells the story of the library and the way that it improves both the cultural and financial life of your community.

The Advocacy Campaign

Sometimes being right just isn't enough. Despite an excellent public awareness campaign and a terrific, high-impact budget presentation, your library may be slated for a level budget, a cut, or even drastic cuts. Forget the fact that other city departments are being cut as well. Don't be taken in by the argument that the town is in a serious budget crisis.

No doubt these arguments are true, but your job is to ensure that the library can deliver excellent services and that means it must have a workable budget. You are not asking for the moon. Remember, in all likelihood, your library takes up less than 4 percent of the operating budget—in most cases, far less. No budget crisis is going to be solved by a reduction say, of 10 percent of the library line item that is less than 4 percent of the city's budget.

And what other city service is offering so much to so many for so little? This is what you have to stay focused on. The library is not part of the city's budget problem, but it can be and has been a contributor to the solution (see the section Public Awareness—Creating the Message on p. 15). If you can't convince the city leaders of this, then perhaps the thousands or hundreds of thousands of residents who use your library can.

Remember, too, that once cut the possibility of easily restoring lost or damaged services is dim indeed—and costly. Significant cuts almost always mean a loss of staff, and as a trustee, you know very well that library services are labor intensive. With the loss of staff will come a loss or at the very least a decline in services. Restoring these services at a later date will also be labor intensive (i.e., costly) because the library administration will have to go through an intensive recruitment and training process to replace lost employees. It's much better to avoid this scenario in the first place.

Timing, as they say, is everything. When you launch your campaign is as important as the campaign itself. So, as you begin to design a campaign, be sure to consider when it will have the greatest possible impact. Your library director will be your best source of information and support here. Perhaps you will be trying to reinstate services that have been cut. Maybe you are anticipating cuts and want to avoid them. Each of these two scenarios dictates timing.

If you are reacting to bad news—a draconian budget cut, for example—you will want to act right away. If you have been reading the paper, working with the library director, and talking to council members, this really shouldn't come as a big surprise. But if cuts mean branch closings, significant reduction in hours, or loss of staff—you should act fast.

If, on the other hand, you see cuts coming well in advance, or if the cuts this year are significant but tolerable but you also expect more cuts next year, then you might be wisest not to act precipitously and, instead, plan for an advocacy campaign just before the budget process next year. Again, your library director can help with the timing.

In a grassroots advocacy campaign, your goal is to get the voters to influence their council members. So, as stated before, you want those who support the library to take action. While planning an advocacy campaign will take some time and dedication, it isn't hard. You will want to create a team to design and implement the campaign but the team itself doesn't need to be exceedingly large. The following are good recruits for the advocacy team:

- Friends leaders
- Foundation members
- Large donors to the library (they don't want to see the value of their gifts reduced by shorter hours or fewer services)

- VIPs in town who have always supported the library
- Trustees, of course

Who should not be on the team (at least not visibly):

- The staff. You should be working closely with the library director behind the scenes on what the library needs for service delivery, what the consequences of the cuts will be, and ensuring that all factual information is accurate. However, in most cases the library staff will be seen as acting in their own interest (at best) and in some cases as being insubordinate if the director reports to city management or the mayor.

This does not mean the staff should not be involved in the public awareness campaign—quite the opposite. The staff is often in the best position to educate their patrons and the community about the value of library services, but this is different. The gloves are now off. The library staff needs to be seen as doing only one thing at this point—providing services.

Once you have your team together, you will have to begin a series of meetings to design your campaign. If you have the luxury of time, you may want to begin planning about three months prior to implementation. There will be behind-the-scenes work to do, so getting started early makes everything easier and smoother.

If you've already determined the timeline for implementation, you are ready to begin discussing strategies to mobilize the public on your behalf. Consider ideas that are easy for the public, because the more work you ask of them, the less likely they are to commit despite all good intentions. Ideas that have worked well for other libraries include those described in the following sections.

Postcard Campaigns

These can be fairly easy to implement, but they do have two downsides. The first is that if you don't get a huge number of postcards sent to council members (or the mayor), then it will look like you have little support and the campaign will backfire. The second is that if there is not some level of effort by the sender (i.e., there is space for the sender to write a personal message), then the postcards will likely be dismissed as a mass (impersonal) mailing.

To resolve the problem of few postcards being mailed, ask the Friends to pay for postage (and even the printing of the cards themselves). A very effective strategy is to have hundreds or thousands of postcards printed, prestamped, and preaddressed. Your team can then recruit a group of volunteers to spend a couple of hours on a Saturday dispersed around town and certainly in front of the library and its branches. They will be tasked with stopping folks and asking them to fill out the postcard and give it back to them. Then, the volunteer should mail the cards. This way you are sure they actually get mailed and you also know exactly how many cards were sent.

If the timing is right, you might partner with the Friends and have them ask everyone at their big book sale to fill out the cards and leave them with the volunteers. Even if your campaign implementation date is several months away, you can save the cards and mail them at the beginning of your campaign.

You know your community and you know where you are likely to get the greatest number of postcards filled out. It may be at a large event or it may take a couple of weekends on the street. The most important thing is to ensure that there are a lot of postcards mailed and that means you mail them yourselves.

Petition Drives

Like the postcard campaign, this is a fairly simple strategy to employ and because of this, it is again imperative that you get a critical mass of signatures. The petition should clearly state what you are asking for—a 10 percent increase in the budget—and in a sentence or two, why; or, if a plea for no cuts again, why. It would also be wise to show on the petition how much money this translates into and how much residents currently pay for services. You want the signers to have the facts, and you want the council to see (when they look at the petitions) that you have given the signers the facts.

As with a postcard campaign, you will have to decide when and where you need volunteers to get the greatest number of signatures possible. Once you have collected the petitions, make sure they are delivered to a council meeting where the press is present—notify the press yourselves of your intent to ensure that you get coverage. You want to be sure that the residents of your community know that there is strong library support and you want the council members to know that the residents know.

Phone Calls

Even more persuasive than postcards and petitions are voter calls to council members directly asking for library funding. This takes more effort than signing a petition or writing a few words on a postcard, so you will want to make it as easy as possible for callers.

If you are asking people to make calls (the entire Friends list should be employed for this purpose) be sure to arm them with a short list of talking points. This keeps everyone on the same page and keeps the request consistent. Also, be sure callers have the phone numbers of those they are to call. The key here is to make it easy for them. One effective strategy is to ask the Friends to pay for an ad on the first day of budget meetings that ask all library supporters to call the mayor at (555) 555-5555 to make the case for library funding.

Op-eds and Letters to the Editor

All your advocacy activities are likely to generate some spontaneous letters to the editor, but you can increase the power of the press by having library-supportive

VIPs write letters. The paper won't publish all of them in most cases, but they will very likely publish those from high-profile residents.

Be sure your volunteer letter writers have those talking points. Make sure they understand exactly what you are asking for—what percentage increase, how much money this means. Make sure they are ready to explain why the library matters and why it is an important investment of resources, especially in hard times. Be sure they know the small percentage of the overall city budget that the library represents. Then let them write their piece.

It is also a good idea to contact the paper's editor and ask if you can have space to place an op-ed. This is an excellent job for the board president. The president has the credentials to know what he or she is talking about. People will respect what the president has to say. Remember, tell the story—show why the library matters to everyone in the community whether they use the library or not.

Mass E-mails to Council Members and/or Mayor

More and more, e-mails are becoming an acceptable form of communication with your local leadership—in many cases, it is the preferred method. If you use this as a way to make your case, be sure that you have a large number of library supporters e-mailing and be sure that everyone uses a subject heading that makes your case clear, such as "Support Library Funding Increase," or "No Cuts to Libraries!" When government leaders get lots and lots of e-mail on a single topic, they will most likely just keep count of those for or against a particular issue, not taking time to read each individual e-mail.

Some Important Points about an Advocacy Campaign

FRIENDS OF THE LIBRARY

If you have a Friends group (and if you don't, you should), be sure to include them in your plans from the very beginning. After all, they are the grassroots and they support the library. Friends should be on the advocacy planning team, and Friends members (even those who aren't active but contribute money) should be called upon to volunteer their time for petition drives, postcard campaigns, and phone calls.

In addition to their help, the Friends can pay for the tools of the campaign. Luckily, the IRS does allow nonprofits to spend money on grassroots advocacy. There is a legal limit on how much they can spend (see Appendix B.14, ALTAFF Statement on Legal Limits of Lobbying for Nonprofits), but your campaign doesn't have to cost a lot to be effective.

THE MEDIA

The media can be your best friend or your worst enemy in your campaign. You can help influence their reaction by letting them in on your plans from the start. Once you've done your preplanning and mapped out your timeline and strategies, and just before you take the campaign public, call the editor of the paper and let him or her know what you're doing and why.

Don't let it be a surprise. Put together a package of information that includes a cover letter about why you find this campaign necessary, your talking points, samples of your petitions and postcards, and any other information that is relevant to your campaign. If you plan to take out an ad in the paper to generate public action, let them know this as well. (It doesn't hurt to let them know you'll be spending money with them in your endeavors—but of course, you don't want to be explicit about it.) Include a name and number where your advocacy team leader can be reached to answer questions.

Finally, understand that despite all your best efforts you may not get what you ask for. You might be successful in reducing the size of a cut or you might get half of the increase you were seeking—these are good outcomes. Realize, though, that you might come away empty-handed. If this happens, take some time to regroup, recognize that you've done your best, and make sure that your public awareness campaign is still in place (and maybe modified based on what you've learned from this experience) for next year.

Capital Campaigns

As communities grow and facilities age, there usually comes a time when a major effort needs to be made to raise a large sum of money for a special purpose; in other words, a capital campaign. The need for major renovations, new construction, or even major new programs (such as new computer labs, a new bookmobile, etc.) often requires a fund-raising campaign. It's true that in some cases, a referendum or a bond issue is passed and that will suffice to raise the funds. At other times, the city council will commit to providing a percentage of the money needed if the rest is raised from the community. And, in some cases, a capital need will only be met through a major fund-raising campaign.

If a capital campaign must be undertaken, there is usually little doubt that it will be spearheaded by the board of trustees. As part of its overall responsibility to ensure that the library has not only the budget and staff needed to provide quality library services, but the infrastructure as well, the board should, ultimately, have final oversight (if not direct involvement) with any major fund-raising campaigns on behalf of the library.

While it is not uncommon for the library's foundation or even Friends group to take on this project, the trustees are ultimately responsible for securing resources needed for library services and should be involved. This involvement can take the form of setting the fund-raising goal, selecting the fund-raising consultant, actively managing the campaign, and volunteering to be solicitors for the campaign.

Whatever the role, the trustees must be involved from the beginning in setting the goal, negotiating a workable timeline, and delegating the campaign's management (if not done by the board itself). In addition, during the campaign, the board must be kept apprised on a regular basis about the progress toward the goal, any unexpected news (good or bad), and problems being faced by the campaign committee and/or volunteers. Finally, each board member must realize that there is a very high expectation that he or she will contribute to the campaign at the highest level possible based on each individual's circumstances.

Once you've decided to embark on a capital campaign, you will need to create a team to manage the process. The board should determine who best to approach for this important volunteer assignment. Ideally, the team should include the following:

- At least one trustee
- At least one member from the library's foundation board (more if the foundation will be taking the lead in the campaign)
- A VIP from the community who will, at the very least, become the honorary chairperson (This well-known and well-respected individual may take only a slight role in the actual work of the campaign, but he or she should be willing to publicly endorse the campaign, provide a quote or quotes for promotional literature, and be willing to be interviewed by the media.)
- A member or members from the Friends executive board
- A member or members from the community who support this campaign and have past fund-raising experience

Believe it or not, there are many people out there who actually enjoy raising money. You may be one of those folks who would rather mortgage your home than ask someone else for a contribution. Luckily, however, there are others who get a genuine thrill and sense of accomplishment when they are able to convince donors to contribute to your worthwhile cause. These are the people who should be on the steering committee and certainly, these are the ones you'll eventually want to recruit to do the actual asking.

Anyone recruited to be on the steering committee should be made well aware that this will be a time-intensive undertaking, and they should understand clearly what their roles will be. This group will have to commit their time not just for the duration of the campaign but for meetings prior to it to map out a plan that will translate into success.

Because this steering committee is so important—the success of your campaign hinges on them—the board will want to have a list of possible names (more than needed since you have to anticipate that a number of those you ask will say no) and will have to commit to asking each person on the list personally.

When recruiting individuals for the steering committee, you should already have determined the following:

- The timeline for the campaign
- The fund-raising goal

- The length of time you'll need their services
- A projected time frame for meetings (There will be many meetings in the beginning even prior to the campaign's kickoff.)
- A list of the types of things you will expect the steering committee to do, such as:
  - Hire a consultant.
  - Work with the consultant to recommend potential high-level donors and to design the campaign itself.
  - Market and promote the campaign.
  - Recruit and manage volunteers who will be out in the field making requests for leadership donations.
  - Manage or oversee a final broad-based or grassroots campaign—the Friends of the library may be the group that takes on this final step.
  - Keep records of the progress, thank donors, and report to the board of trustees as the campaign progresses.
  - Do a postmortem on the campaign—win or lose, it will be important for future library fund-raising to have an account of what worked and what didn't.

Hiring a Fund-Raising Consultant

Once the steering committee has been pulled together, the first order of business should be hiring a good consultant. In a small community, there may be a volunteer who has waged a successful capital campaign before, and may be willing to volunteer or be hired to consult for your campaign. In all probability, however, you will want to develop a request for proposals (RFP) to find the person or firm that you are confident will help your campaign be successful.

So, what will you look for in a consultant? Unfortunately, you won't be looking for someone who will go out and raise the money for you. First of all, legitimate consultants do not do this, and second, the large donations you will be seeking will be given by those in your community who believe in the library and believe in the credibility of the person asking. This will be a person they know or know of and it will be another person from the community who has already given to the campaign.

You will be looking for a consultant who has been successful before, has excellent references, who understands the importance and value of libraries to the community, and who has connected with the members of the committee on a personal level. You want to be sure that the consultant you hire is a person you trust and like—you'll be working with him or her intensely for a good period of time.

A fund-raising consultant should be expected to help you develop a case statement, determine the feasibility of your goal, investigate the potential of the large donors you list as possible contributors to give at the level the committee estimates, help develop a campaign strategy that includes the various gift levels that will be needed to ensure you meet your goal, help the committee develop a successful strategy for marketing, and help you train the volunteers who will be making the requests of individuals for donations—called "making the ask."

Finding the Right Consultant

So, what do you need to know to find and then hire the best consultant for your campaign? The following is a list of steps the board and/or the steering committee will want to follow:

- Create a list of possible consultants. This can be done by asking other local agencies who they used for successful campaigns, asking around locally for good suggestions, and checking the AFP (Association of Fundraising Professionals) directory or other fund-raising directories.

- Create an RFP (the city's purchasing department may be able to help you with this). The RFP should tell a little about your library, your need for the campaign, and how much you wish to raise along with the ideal qualifications of the person or firm selected. Ask respondents to include their fee schedule (avoid those who ask for a percentage of the money raised—this is not the standard professional practice), an estimated timeline for the campaign, and an outline of services that the respondents will provide within the fee structure.

- Send the RFP to six or eight firms or individual consultants from the list you have established and give them a deadline for response.

- After you receive the responses, select the top three you think are best suited for the project and set up times for interviewing the top three.

- Let the other respondents who are qualified but who didn't make the top three know that you have selected the first round of applicants for interviews. Let them know that you will contact them if your first round doesn't produce the consultant you want.

- Send thank-you letters to those who are not qualified and let them know that they have not been selected. It is considered a courtesy to tell these people why they were not selected.

Interviewing Prospective Consultants

When you have scheduled the top three consultants or consulting firms, you will want to be sure that your interviews with them are comprehensive—this will help you avoid unpleasant surprises once you've made the hiring decision. Also, you will want to be sure that you ask each of the top three contenders the same questions so that you are making clear and consistent comparisons between them.

The following are issues that should be discussed during each interview:

- How will you work with the steering committee and its volunteers during the course of the campaign? What do you expect the steering committee to provide to help you in your work?

- What specific services do you provide within the scope of your stated fee?
  - A campaign plan? What will this include?
  - An assessment of our goal and its viability?
  - Regular written reports?
  - Campaign materials?
  - Training for our solicitors?
  - Support for marketing the campaign?
  - Support throughout the campaign?
  - Help following the campaign in wrapping things up?
  - Are travel expenses additional and, if so, what is the estimated cost of these?

- What similar campaigns have you been involved in recently and what was their level of success?

- What is your initial response about the viability of our goal and how much time do you think it will take to achieve it?

- What is the billing schedule? (Fees should always be based on services rendered and not on a contingency of the funds raised.)

- How many people are in your firm and who, specifically, will be dealing with us on a regular basis? (Remember, you want to be working with someone you like and trust, so if the principals of a firm have come for the interview but the person you'll actually be working with is someone else, you will have to schedule a second interview with that person.)

- If the goal is not met or if the campaign is halted for some reason, what is your policy regarding unpaid fees or refunds?

- If we want extra services beyond the contract, what is your charge for change orders?

Making the Decision

Once the interviews are complete, the steering committee will have to make an important decision and it shouldn't be done lightly. The consultant you select will be a key to your success, so there is much to consider, including these factors:

- **Chemistry**. This is not as trivial as it might sound. You have to be comfortable with the person who will be intimately involved with your campaign and your committee.

- **Experience**. How many campaigns has the consultant been involved with and what has been the level of their success?

- **Deliverables**. What will you be getting from the consultant and what will you have to develop yourselves—such as campaign materials, marketing strategies, and volunteer training?

- **Cost**. Not the first consideration by a long shot, but if there is a significant difference in fees and you like the second choice fairly well, you should either (1) try to negotiate the cost down with your first choice, or (2) consider, instead, the second choice.

- **References**. This is critical. Be sure to get three recent references for agencies with whom the consultant has worked. Follow up with these references and make sure you find out:
  - If the fund-raising goal was met
  - What the consultant provided
  - Whether the reference would hire the consultant again
  - What advice the reference would give you about working with this consultant

When you have made the final selection, get a contract that outlines and verifies what services you'll be receiving, what will be provided by the steering committee, an enumeration of the on-site visits you can expect, the full costs for services, a timeline for completion, a billing schedule, an explanation of any extra costs—what might incur them and how much they'll be—and an explanation of refunds (if any) should the campaign be stopped, if the consultant fails to deliver services, or if the campaign is unsuccessful. This will be boilerplate on the consultant's end, so just be sure you go over it carefully (having an attorney look at it is a prudent idea) because it will be written to protect the consultant and not necessarily you.

Finally, you should notify the other candidates you interviewed and tell them which consultant you selected and why. Also, if you've kept a second tier of potential consultants on hold, you should now notify them as well.

No library can be successful without having the financial resources it needs for the operating budget, for continuing maintenance, and occasionally for a major building project. Governing boards of trustees have fiduciary responsibilities and that means that they must ensure that the budget is secure and that capital and/or advocacy campaigns are launched when necessary.

3

Critical but Different Roles: The Library's Board and Its Director

The library's director is undoubtedly the single most important key to its success. An excellent library director works well with the trustees, the staff, local government, and the community. Because the quality of this person will impact that quality of library services, it's imperative that the board works to create the best working relationship possible. This means that they take time to hire exactly the right person when the opportunity presents itself; they provide support and guidance by way of honest and productive evaluations; and they are clear about their respective roles.

Nothing will ruin a good working relationship faster than a board micromanaging the director or a director who does not communicate clearly with the trustees, providing them with all the information they need to make good decisions within their prescribed roles. If you are experiencing significant turnover in the position of library director, you may want to consider whether or not you are acting as a governing board or if you are crossing the lines into management.

To ensure that your board is working effectively with the library director, you should engage in a self-evaluation exercise (see Chapter 6). This will give each trustee an opportunity to critically evaluate their understanding of what they are responsible for as trustees and where the library director's responsibilities lie.

Understanding Respective Roles

Understanding the difference between governance and management is not always easy. There are gray areas, and when they occur they can create ill will if not sorted out. If there are areas that are really not clear-cut, a board might ask themselves who will be held ultimately accountable for the outcome. Will the director look like he or she is not competent if a particular idea regarding the library's services doesn't work? Will he or she be held accountable? If so, it is only right to leave the implementation of ideas or goals in his or her hands.

Following are categories in which both the board and the director will be involved. Under each category are generally accepted role descriptions that can help delineate who is responsible for what.

General Administration

TRUSTEES

The board of trustees does not manage the library or become involved in daily operational issues. If the board is a governing board, however, they do hire and then evaluate the library director based on the effectiveness of the programs and services of the library. Because the library director is ultimately responsible for the design and implementation of services as well as oversight and evaluation of staff, he or she must have full responsibility and accountability for them.

The governing board should be very knowledgeable about the library's mission and goals so that it can evaluate the library director appropriately in meeting them. As a part of the library director's evaluation, the board should work with him or her in developing a yearly performance plan for each succeeding year.

An advisory board of trustees (one without the authority to hire or fire the director) may not have input into the evaluation of the library director because typically, if the library is a city or county department, that evaluation will be made by the city or county administrator. The advisory board, however, can be extremely useful in providing both ideas and feedback on how the library and library director is doing in fulfilling its mission.

LIBRARY DIRECTOR

If the library director is hired by the trustees, he or she is directly under their governance and is ultimately answerable to them. If, however, the library director is hired by the city or town and the library is a municipal department, the library director will be answerable to city officials, and the board may well be advisory only. In either case, however, the director is responsible for the day-to-day management and decision making at the library within the library's policy framework. When the library director is hired by the municipality, his or her evaluation will be made by city administrators. When the library director is hired by the trustees, he or she will be evaluated by the board and will serve at their pleasure.

The library director in both cases (above) meets with the trustees on a regular basis and reports on the state of the library including budget, programs, services, and library use. It is also important for the library director to share with the trustees the outlook for the library's needs and resources as well as other issues that currently or may ultimately affect library services. Keeping the trustees fully informed about challenges and opportunities on the horizon will allow the trustees (whether advisory or governing) to be well-informed advocates for the library.

Policy

TRUSTEES

Library policy provides the framework within which the library operates. It gives guidance to the library director in making decisions about programs, services, and staff management and development. Working with the library director to develop and then adopt library policy is one of the trustees' most important roles. While it is likely that the library director and his or her staff will initially draft needed policy statements (or recommend specific modifications to existing policies), the trustees should thoroughly understand each policy, understand why it is important and necessary, and stand ready to support it.

LIBRARY DIRECTOR

Though it is ultimately the trustees who officially adopt library policy (this is often true for advisory boards as well, depending on state laws governing library policy), the trustees will depend heavily on the library director for the formulation of policy. Because the library director is in the best position to understand the issues that impact and will be impacted by library policy—for example, legal, financial, service quality—he or she should work with appropriate staff to draft policy statements to present to the trustees.

In addition, the library director should prepare background papers or white papers to share with the trustees so that they will understand the context for the policy, the issues the policy will effectively address, and the pros and cons of the proposed policy. With this background information, the trustees will be in a better position to ask insightful questions, make useful modifications, and ultimately adopt the policy, which they now fully understand and can stand behind.

Strategic Planning

TRUSTEES

Though it is likely that the library director will coordinate the planning process, the trustees should ensure that it happens. The trustees can initiate the process, work with the library director to design an overview of the process, and then participate as needed as the planning takes place.

The board of trustees is ultimately responsible to see the library's mission is carried out and should ensure that the programs and services the library director develops respond to and forward the library's mission. As citizen representatives to the library and (in the case of a governing board) answerable to the public for the good stewardship of it as a community resource, the trustees should support library service that is responsive to community needs by overseeing the process.

LIBRARY DIRECTOR

One of the most important jobs for the library director is to manage the planning process. The library director is in the best position to coordinate the process and should have the best insight about the emerging environment within which the library operates. The planning process should include the staff and the trustees, as well as the Friends, who can provide wonderful insight and ideas for serving the end users. It may be the trustees who initiate the planning process, but because this process will involve so many and take appreciable time, the library director will most likely be the lead individual. This does not mean, of course, that the library director will be involved in all stages or ultimately decide what the plan will look like, but he or she will and should be in charge of the process.

Marketing

TRUSTEES

Trustees can and should be frontline ambassadors for the library. They should be well aware of the library's marketing plan and be an important component of its implementation. Members of the board of trustees can play an invaluable role in giving input into the library's marketing campaign, making sure that it resonates with the general public.

Trustees who are well educated about the library's marketing plan are well armed to go out to other civic and cultural groups and to public officials to discuss the importance and value of the library and to encourage greater use and support. Each trustee should consider such outreach services part of his or her job description.

LIBRARY DIRECTOR

Effective marketing requires a clear understanding of what services the library offers and why it matters. Optimally, the entire library support system—director, staff, trustees, and Friends—should be involved in library marketing and promotion. Some libraries have public relations staff in-house, and this staff, under the direction of the library director, develops marketing campaigns.

The trustees should be well aware of the marketing strategy, give input into its development, and should help implement the campaign through speaking engagements, letters to the editor, and whatever support is possible. The Friends, too, can and should participate in the campaign. They might wish to develop compatible materials to promote both the library and Friends membership. In addition, they may well help finance the campaign and, of course, they can be excellent ambassadors of the campaign. When there is no public relations staff available, the library director should involve the trustees and Friends members even more heavily in the development and implementation of the campaign.

Fiscal

TRUSTEES

Governing boards (those who have the authority to hire/fire and evaluate the director) are responsible for adopting the budget that is submitted for authorization.

They are responsible for understanding its components as well as the impact that the budget has on the overall delivery of library services.

Both governing and advisory boards of trustees should be the most visible advocates of the budget, ensuring that it passes and that the resources the library needs to deliver effective services are secured. This may include visits with city or county administrators, making the case for the library's budget publicly, and possibly even generating grassroots support for the library's budget.

While this work is generally most intense at budget time, the trustees should be visible proponents of good library funding throughout the year (see the section Marketing on p. 34). Though the library director takes the lead, the trustees must be involved as the budget is developed and educated about what it takes to provide services. This is especially important if it is a governing board, as these members have legal fiduciary responsibilities to ensure that public monies are being well spent in support of library services. In addition, if the trustees are not well-informed, consulted, and in agreement with the final product, they cannot be the effective advocates they must be for its final adoption.

LIBRARY DIRECTOR

The library's budget is the best tool the library director has to implement services and move the library's long (and short) range plans forward. Nobody knows better than the director what staff positions, equipment, collection enhancements, programs, and so on are needed to provide quality service and what each element of service costs. The development of the library's budget is a chief responsibility of the director, and because the director will be evaluated on performance that is inextricably linked to the resources available to implement services, he or she should have the most responsibility for the budget that the board of trustees either adopts themselves (governing) or delivers to the fiscal authorities for its adoption. As part of fiscal planning, the library director should also consider what resources may be available from the Friends in the coming year for items that are not normally a standard part of the operating budget, and present a wish list to the Friends for possible funding.

Legislative/Advocacy

TRUSTEES

Advocacy is an important role for all trustees because ensuring that the library has the funding it needs to effectively serve the community is paramount. While engaging in good public relations on behalf of the library should be an ongoing effort, advocacy campaigns are geared to achieving a specific goal— avoiding budget cuts or securing budget increases, passing a bond referendum, encouraging support for a building initiative, and so on. Trustees, as the citizen leaders of the library, should be the leaders in advocacy as well. Working with guidance from the library director and with the support and assistance of the Friends, trustees can and should work to make the library a high priority for funding.

In addition to advocacy at the local level, trustees should be aware of state and national issues that can and will affect their library. State and national legislative leaders should hear from library trustees on these issues when they arise. Always, a personal visit is best, but participation in letter writing campaigns, phone call campaigns, and other advocacy campaigns are also critically important.

LIBRARY DIRECTOR

The library director's role in advocacy and legislative initiatives on behalf of the library can be a little tricky. If the director serves at the pleasure of the city or county authorities (and the library is a department of that entity), he or she will most likely be extremely limited in how visible he or she can be in advocacy efforts at the local level—especially as it relates to budget increases.

The director, however, must be involved in all advocacy efforts (at least behind the scenes) to ensure that others such as the trustees and Friends are well aware of what is at stake in getting the resources the library needs.

An effective advocacy campaign is dependent on a well-articulated and consistent message about what the library needs and why it matters. No one can answer these questions better than the director. When the library director cannot actively participate in a campaign, he or she should be sure that the trustees and Friends are the visible advocates and that they have all the information they need to be effective.

When the library is a separate agency governed by the trustees, the library director can be much more visible in promoting the library's legislative and fiscal agenda. Even though the director should be the lead person with providing information for trustees and Friends, he or she will be much more effective by empowering the trustees and Friends to be the visible leaders of any campaign so that there won't be the appearance of self-interest. This is also true for state and national advocacy and legislative initiatives since library supporters and volunteers (Friends and trustees) have weightier voices and, of course, they have the sheer numbers to make the case at all levels of government.

Meetings

TRUSTEES

Attending regular meetings with the library administration is the best opportunity library trustees have to keep up to date and be fully educated on library services, programs, concerns, and issues. Trustees should require that they receive "board packets" from their library director at least one week in advance. The job of the trustee is to read the information in the packet and come to the meeting ready to discuss the items therein. For the benefit of the library, trustees who find that they must miss more than two meetings each year or who are unable to read materials ahead of the meeting should resign so that someone who has the time to do so can be appointed in their place.

Working with the library director, the board president is responsible for developing an agenda and presiding over the meeting, ensuring that each item gets the attention it needs while also making sure that all members present have a chance to participate. For effective communication and relations between the Friends and the trustees, it is a good idea to include a Friends update on each agenda and ask that the Friends appoint a liaison who can come and give a brief report. To keep the meetings productive, the president should ensure that no one person dominates the meeting and that meetings end on time.

LIBRARY DIRECTOR

The library director facilitates regular trustee meetings (typically once a month). In this role, the director supports the trustees in developing the agenda, providing background information for substantive discussion on each of the agenda items, whether action items or discussion items. The director should ensure that each trustee gets a board packet that includes year-to-date use statistics, background on any action or discussion items, a budget report, and a report on library programs and services for the month. The packet is important information for the ongoing education of the trustees about the library, its services and utilization, and the effectiveness of its resources. The board packet should be made available to the trustees at least one week in advance of meetings so they have time to go over it and formulate questions and comments ahead of the meeting.

In addition to attending every meeting of the trustees, the library director or his or her designee should also attend every meeting of the Friends. The best way for the director to ensure that the Friends can effectively help support the library's goals is to ensure a library presence at each meeting. In the best-case scenario, the library director will be the one to attend the meetings (an important element of development, which is an important role for the director). If the director cannot attend these meetings, he or she should appoint a high-ranking member of the library's administration. The director should ask the Friends to include time for the library administrator to report out at each meeting and to include the Friends in discussions about the library's goals. The library director or staff should never be a voting member of the Friends' board in order to avoid any appearance of a conflict of interest.

Networking

TRUSTEES

A great way to ensure that advocacy and public awareness campaigns succeed is to build connections with those who make a difference for the library all year round. Set a goal to be on a first-name basis with the mayor by attending city events and introducing yourself. Send letters and e-mails to local VIPs to thank them for specific efforts they've made on behalf of the city—even those efforts that have nothing to do with the library. Same goes for your state representatives. Trustees should recognize that their important position in the community provides a level of entrée to other civic leaders that they should exploit.

LIBRARY DIRECTOR

Sometimes the old adage is really true—it's not what you know but who you know. The library director can garner significant political clout for the library by networking with local community leaders, as well as state and national legislators. Attending and meeting with government leaders at state and national legislative days is a good way to begin making inroads with those who can affect library finances and policies. In addition, meeting and corresponding with state and national leaders throughout the year can help raise the profile of both the director and the library.

In addition to political clout, one of the best ways for a library director to keep up with library trends and best practices is to be actively involved in library associations at all levels and attend library workshops and conferences. If funding for the attendance at state and national meetings is not included in the budget, the Friends should be prevailed upon to support this important avenue for continuing education.

Hiring and Evaluating the Library Director

Find an excellent library and you will have found an excellent library director. Unfortunately, the reverse is also true. A library that is stagnant, unfriendly, low profile, and just plain dowdy most assuredly has a director who is well past his or her "retire by" date, is the opposite of dynamic, does not have the respect of the staff, is not a leader in the community, or just isn't management or leadership material.

Because the quality of library service can be directly linked to the director, it is critical for the board to hire the right person, provide support and growth potential through the evaluation process, and, if all else fails, fire a director who is not living up to the goals you mutually set and who is not moving the library to center stage in the community. If a board fails at this job, it has failed the community—it's really that important.

Hiring a New Director

Though it does take time and effort, hiring a new library director is a real opportunity to get an enthusiastic person who can bring new perspectives and ideas to bear on the library's services. This will only happen, however, if the board has a good idea about what type of person and qualifications they want in a director. If staff morale is low, they may be looking for someone who has a great background in staff development. Maybe you have a major building project on the horizon and want someone who has experience in this area. Perhaps you are ready to embark on a capital campaign and want excellent fund-raising skills.

These will all be important considerations, but remember, once the funds are raised, the staff morale is high, and the buildings are built, you still have the same director. You should be careful that your immediate needs don't weigh too heavily in your selection. Someone with a great building background, for example, but doesn't have good human relations skills will be wonderful in the short term but may cause serious staff problems in the future and may fail to be the community leader you want and need for the long term.

It is probably best to look for intelligence, energy, passion, and experience. A smart and energetic director will come up to snuff on building issues soon enough (and if you are building, you should have a building consultant). Learning how to engage in fund-raising isn't hard and an intelligent and passionate director will fit right in. People skills, charisma, energy, and intelligence can't be taught, so consider weighing your decision more heavily in favor of those traits and characteristics that make mere managers into leaders.

Many larger library systems hire professionals to conduct the job search, which is fine. These library consultants are well networked—they can prescreen applicants who meet your needs and save the board a lot of time. They can help you design an excellent position description and advertisement, and they will take care of posting the ads and narrowing the field for board interviews. They will also check references and help with any follow-up necessary.

Failing a professional library consultant or firm, a large board can create a task force to conduct the search. The task force should realize that there will be time involved but that the process is very interesting and it is the most important one any board can perform. A small board can act as a whole and create the advertisements, screen candidate applications, set up interviews, do all the interviewing themselves, and check on references.

POSITION DESCRIPTION

Before you can even begin to advertise for a new director, you will have to do some homework. The first item of business should be a review of the position description for the director. Get it out and make sure it truly reflects what you are looking for. The position description should include educational qualifications and experience requirements, but it should also include those intangibles like leadership qualities, commitment to intellectual freedom, a willingness to work with staff in a team environment, and the ability to be a community leader. Figure 3.1 is a fine example from the Omaha (Nebraska) Public Library.

SALARY CONSIDERATIONS

So often the old adage is true—you get what you pay for. This isn't always the case in hiring. Sometimes the ideal candidate is from the area and wants to stay or return; sometimes he or she will see this as a good career move if coming from a

---

**Figure 3.1. Library Director Position Description,
Omaha Public Library (Omaha, NE)**

Library Director: Omaha Public Library

Primary Responsibility:

To plan, direct and manage the Omaha Public Library System and lead it to strategic success and fulfillment of identified objectives. The Director will coordinate services and activities with the Board of Library Trustees and other City departments, divisions and outside agencies, and must exercise considerable initiative, independent judgment and political acumen to ensure that library services complement the needs and desires of community residents.

Essential Duties:

Vision and Strategic Leadership

- To establish, with the Board of Trustees, and to implement a long-range vision that aligns the library's mission, goals and objectives with community needs and City priorities. To lead staff and other stakeholders toward achieving the vision.
- To develop and execute strategies and programs to increase visibility and support for the Library, including advocacy, promotional and educational campaigns to improve understanding and optimize use of library system programs and resources.
- To develop and implement, in conjunction with the Mayor's Office and Library Board of Trustees, the Library's Strategic Plan in response to community needs, priorities and resources.

OPL Organizational Culture

- To create and evolve a passionate, progressive and dynamic organizational culture.
- To provide leadership to attract, recruit and develop high-performance professional and support staff.
- To instill a customer service culture geared toward improving both library services and customer satisfaction with the library's materials, services and facilities.
- To determine appropriate staffing levels, work performance standards, to correct deficiencies and implement discipline and termination procedures.

Community Leadership and Engagement

- To establish mutually beneficial working relationships with The Nebraska Library Commission and other regional consortia through participation in professional organizations, to create opportunities to showcase OPL and further OPL's mission.
- To communicate and engage with the media, community groups, Foundation and Friends' organizations and the public to inform and garner support for OPL's vision, programs and fund-raising.

OPL System Operations and Management

- To develop and implement, in conjunction with the Mayor's Office and Library Board of Trustees, a sound financial plan for current and future library operations including cultivating grants, private funding sources and endowments in cooperation with the Library Foundation.
- To oversee and direct the library budget in a fiscally sound manner consistent with City resources and priorities.
- To oversee the development and maintenance of library buildings. To provide leadership for major development projects, including strategic and tactical reviews of OPL System facility requirements and construction and renovation of facilities.

(Continued)

**Figure 3.1. Library Director Position Description,
Omaha Public Library (Omaha, NE) (Continued)**

OPL System Operations and Management (Continued)

- To stay abreast of new trends and innovations in the fields of library administration and management and integrate best practices into the management and culture of OPL.

Requirements:

- A Master's degree in Library Science from a Library School program accredited by the American Library Association.
- A Minimum of seven years of increasingly responsible library management experience.
- Proven experience in successful community stakeholder engagement, including with City political and administrative bodies, community organizations, support groups and community residents.
- Excellent leadership, communication, conflict resolution and coaching skills.

---

smaller library, and it could be that your ideal candidate really doesn't care that much about salary.

It's important to realize, however, that when recruiting for the best, you have to offer your best salary range. If your salary range is already set by the city but isn't consistent with what other library directors are getting in your area, you have some work to do with the city leaders to get the range up, but in the meantime, if you are stuck with a range, you may want to advertise that the salary is "up to $75,000" rather than advertising that the starting range is "$62,500 to $75,000 depending on qualifications." Let the highest number be the one that will bring in the best and the most experienced.

If your board sets the salary, take a look at the current range and compare it to salaries offered by similar-sized libraries in your region. If at all possible, make your range slightly higher. Candidates looking in your region will take note. Even if an increase in the director's salary causes a decrease in other line items, do it. Remember, the library director is the single most important resource your library has. A good library director will help you get good budgets, keep morale high, use innovative methods to stretch the budget, and will be seen as a leader in the community—bringing the library into even higher profile.

If your salary range isn't as competitive as you wish and there isn't much you can do to change that immediately, you might consider expanding the benefits. More paid time off can be a very attractive lure for some potential candidates, and it doesn't directly affect your bottom line. Be creative to entice as many candidates as possible and think of additional benefits in lieu of a higher salary that you can offer.

ADVERTISING

Pretty much all advertising for library positions is done online these days. However, the sources for the ads are still the same, with the exception of sites such as Monster.com. If you are conducting a national search, you will want to include online ads in national journals such as *American Libraries* and *Library Journal*. Regardless of size, you will want to place ads with the state library association and the state library. You might also consider the associations and state libraries of neighboring states to expand the search. Be sure, too, to let prospective applicants know that you'll pay for their travel and expenses if they are selected for an interview.

Regardless of the size of your library, you will want to cast your net as widely as possible. You are looking for the perfect director, and that person may live across the state or across the country. The more qualified people who see your ad, the more likely you'll be to find the perfect person for your library.

A word about "general" online job sites: Because you are looking for a professional librarian with experience and specific education, you might want to think twice about these sites. What experience has shown is that you will get hundreds, if not thousands, of responses—few if any from qualified applicants. Professional librarians seeking new positions will be checking the national library journals and, if they are interested in your area of the country, they will be checking the state library sites as well. You are not likely to miss a qualified applicant by foregoing general sites.

Writing up your job advertisement won't be that difficult if you have reviewed and updated the position description. Depending on the price structure for online ads, you may be able to post the entire job description along with the minimum requirements and the salary. If there are limits on word counts, you can save money by drawing up an abbreviated version. Just be sure to include the qualities you are looking for and be sure to sell this as the best position in the world. What are the opportunities for a new director? What is so special about your town? Why is this library a perfect choice for a career move? Figure 3.2 is an excellent example.

SCREENING APPLICANTS

If you've done a good job in advertising, you will have to go through a lot of résumés and cover letters. You can begin by ruling out anyone who doesn't meet the minimum requirements—having an MLS from an American Library Association–accredited school, for example. Regarding experience, you might consider being a little open minded here. Too often a library will prefer someone who has many years of experience in similar-sized libraries. Sometimes, though, the real go-getters will come from smaller systems or have experience only as an assistant director or a department head. When you are looking through those résumés, consider excellent qualities and accomplishments along with years and type of experience.

If at all possible, narrow the field down to the top three to four candidates for interviews. You can hold back some who narrowly miss the cut for a second round of interviews if necessary, but if you try to interview too many, you will forget what you liked and didn't like about Candidate 1 after interviewing Candidate 5—even

---

Figure 3.2. Library Director Position Description, Patten Free Library (Bath, ME)

Patten Free Library
33 Summer Street
Bath, Maine 04530
(207) 443-5141

Serving the City of Bath and the communities of Arrowsic, Georgetown, Phippsburg, West Bath, and Woolwich for over 150 years

Employment Opportunity: Library Director

The Board of Trustees of the Patten Free Library seeks an experienced, energetic Director to lead its award-winning program serving the city of Bath, Maine and the five adjacent towns of Arrowsic, Phippsburg, Georgetown, West Bath, and Woolwich. A registered 501(c)(3) non-profit, the Patten Free Library is a private organization providing public library services to approximately 17,500 residents of midcoast Maine. 42% of the library's annual budget of $700,000 comes from endowment, 42% from municipal contributions, and the remaining 16% from various fund-raising activities including a library bookstore and annual appeal.

The Library has a staff of five full-time professional Librarians and numerous, highly credentialed part-time employees with a strong commitment to patron service. An active Friends group and an energetic cadre of volunteers also serve the Library. Founded in 1847, Patten Free Library has a striking 19th century building and two modern additions anchoring beautiful Library Park in the center of Bath's federally recognized Historic District.

Responsibilities of the Director

1. Report monthly to a Board of Trustees composed of members elected by the Corporators as well as representatives appointed by the municipalities and the regional school unit.

2. Present an annual budget, oversee all budgetary transactions, and plan annual fund-raising activities.

3. Supervise full and part-time staff, providing annual evaluations, training, work schedules, etc., as well as recommending wage and salary levels.

4. Lead the staff in maintaining the Library's reputation for superior patron service.

5. Lead the staff in planning and implementing public programs for all ages.

6. Partner with the Friends of the Library in planning volunteer activities to benefit Patten Free Library.

7. Be a highly visible public advocate for the Patten Free Library with the media, municipalities, and the library community at large.

8. Monitor the Library's building and grounds, and arrange and supervise all maintenance, repair, and improvements to same.

9. Conduct the planning necessary to help the Patten Free Library meet the changing needs of its patrons for materials and services.

Qualifications

1. An MLS degree from an ALA-accredited institution and a minimum of five years of progressively responsible experience in library services and management.

(Continued)

**Figure 3.2. Library Director Position Description,
Patten Free Library (Bath, ME) (Continued)**

Qualifications *(Continued)*

2. A proven track record of budget management and fund-raising success in keeping with the distinctive funding sources of the Patten Free Library.

3. Extensive personnel management experience that empowers staff and specific experience with a personnel evaluation model based on mutually agreed-upon, on-going, attainable, and measurable goals and objectives.

4. Ability to present the Library's mission, objectives, and fiscal needs to all elements of its constituency—patrons, volunteers, donors, civic leaders, elected officials, media, government agencies, and private foundations, as well as state and national library organizations.

5. Demonstrated command of best library practices, trends, and planning techniques.

6. Ability to administer the Library using current and future technologies and a desire to keep the Patten Free Library in the forefront of technological service to its staff and patrons.

7. Ability to manage the changing environment of patron needs and fiscal realities by envisioning the future role of the library and initiating the steps necessary to fulfill this vision.

Compensation

A salary no less than $55,000 per annum, depending on experience, with a full benefit package and annual vacation.

Application Process

Individuals interested in this position should submit a cover letter, resume, references, and a short essay (not to exceed 500 words) on the challenges facing libraries in the 21st century to searchcommittee@patten.lib.me.us.

Review of applications begins in mid-August and will continue until the position is filled. The Search Committee expects to have the Director in place no later than 1 January 2010.

---

if you've written everything down. It can go back to those important intangibles like charisma, energy, and passion.

To narrow down the field, you can consider developing a rubric that delineates the various qualifications you are looking for and assigns a numeric value to each. With such a tool, you can get a little closer to quantifying the differences between candidates. Truly, though, many qualities, though they can be prioritized by a rubric system, will be subjectively rated by those involved in the interviewing process. That said, it makes sense to always use judgment and perception as well as any numeric rating your interviewing team may come up with.

When you have gone through the résumés and made the first-round selection, you should write to those who were at the bottom of the list and let them know they have not been selected for interviews. If you have a backup list of those who narrowly missed the first cut, wait to contact them after the interviews. If the process has netted you a new director, you can send regret letters at that time.

If the top candidates didn't seem perfect to you, you can call this group in to interview next.

Whether you received lots of applications or not enough, there sometimes are times when you need to reopen your search. You won't want to because this can be an exhausting process, but if you don't find just the person you were hoping for, don't act in haste and repent in leisure. Reconsider the salary you are offering and the perks. Can you add to vacation time? Can you offer continuing education? Can you get the salary up a little higher? Did you cast your net wide enough? These are all the considerations the interview team will have to discuss.

If you are truly exhausted and at a loss for where to go from here, consider hiring that library consultant you thought you just couldn't afford. Look at all the money you've saved by going without a director. Even a small library will benefit by the network of prospects that consultants provide, and they will help you market the position to pull in the right people for consideration.

THE INTERVIEW

The interview process is the very best chance you have to determine whether any of the candidates is the right person for you. By now you have sorted through cover letters and résumés and have determined that each of the people you'll be interviewing meet your minimum qualifications—on paper.

Before you begin scheduling the interviews, you should design the interview process. This will include not only a list of questions you'll be asking each candidate, but should also include a tour of the facilities—at least the main library if you are a larger system. You might also wish to set up interviews or meet and greets with some of the senior staff members so you can get their feedback in the process. If this is to be a day-long process, you should consider taking each candidate to lunch (this is a chance to visit with them on an informal basis and get a better idea about their personality and confidence), or you could ask members of the senior staff to do so. Along with this broader introduction to your library and some members of the staff, you'll be conducting that all-important interview.

During the formal interview, you'll be fleshing out some of the information you've gathered on the résumé, digging deeper into the professional philosophies of each candidate, and getting a better understanding of their approach to services, staff, and community. You've seen their written communication skills in their cover letters—and to an extent, their résumés—now you'll have a chance to assess each individual's communications skills as well.

Because each candidate is different with different experiences, some questions will be tailored specifically to individuals. It's important, however, that the bulk of the questions you ask each candidate are the same so that you can compare responses to the same inquiries. It's important that you have developed a list of open-ended questions that allow for each candidate to expound on his or her answers.

There are some questions that have become so routine that all the interview books coach job applicants on how to answer them best. Because these have become so pat, you can save some time eschewing the typical interview questions and ask questions that get to the heart of each candidate's commitment to library service in all its ramifications.

For example, if you ask candidates to tell about their greatest strength and weakness, you will no doubt get the formulated (and usually highly fictional) response that their great weakness is impatience because the world doesn't always move at their fast rate, and their greatest strength is impatience because they can really get things done. In other words, their greatest weakness is a strength. This will be the response in almost every case and it's meaningless. The following, instead, are open-ended questions that can really delve into professional beliefs, values, and management styles.

- **What is the library philosophy that guides your practice and decision making?** This will probably take many candidates by surprise. It's a good first question for that reason because anyone who has taken time to read and contemplate the value of libraries and how practice and services align with this value will love the question. They'll do a good job of responding. Those who haven't given this much thought will be a little stymied for sure. You want a library director that can articulate his or her philosophy and one who depends on this foundation to make decisions on collection development, staffing, outreach services, and bringing the library to the forefront of the community.

- **In developing a budget proposal for the board, what would guide your priorities for service?** This is a chance to see what is most important to each candidate for service delivery. Is it reaching out to underserved populations and therefore, outreach staffing is a priority? This could be especially important if your community is highly diverse and there are clear class distinctions in educational opportunities and access. Is it making sure that library users are always able to get exactly what they want every time they come to the library and therefore, popular collections would get the highest priority? This again could have implications depending on whether your community is homogenous (if that's really true anywhere) or again, diverse with underserved populations. In short, this question will tell you where the candidate's service values are.

- **What interests you in this job particularly and why?** It's always good to know what someone's motivation is. Perhaps some candidates want to move back to their home—the area in which they were raised or still have family. Perhaps you are embarking on a building project and a candidate would love to be involved with that. Perhaps yours is an urban library and the candidate wants the opportunity to provide services to traditional nonusers as well as more traditional library users. The answer to this question can give you a little insight into what is important to each candidate.

- **In what ways do you involve your staff in the planning process?** This can give the interviewing team an idea of how much a candidate delegates and how involved he or she would like the staff to be. It would be interesting to see if the candidate expounds on this response and talks about including trustees and Friends as well. If not, asking about this is a good follow-up question.

- **What kinds of activities would you engage in to market and highlight the library to the community and why (if at all) is marketing library services important?** In this day and age, it would be unlikely to find a candidate for library director who doesn't think raising the library's profile in the community is important, but it will be most interesting to find out why. Is it simply to bring in more people to the library? If so, why is that important? Is it to bring about a better understanding of the library's value to the community? Again, why does that matter? This is a good open-ended question and will tell you a lot about a candidate's vision for public awareness about the library.

- **In what ways does intellectual freedom promote access, and where might you draw the line on specific materials?** Might as well know now if the candidate disagrees with putting Internet filters on computers for children, because access is the most important issue of all, or if a candidate would put the swimsuit issue of *Sports Illustrated* on a closed shelf. There is no doubt that your library and your community adhere to certain values and cultures regarding this issue. That doesn't mean that the preferred candidate has to agree with the traditional culture, but if he or she is way outside of where you know the board stands, it could become an important factor.

In the end, you are looking for the intelligence and qualities that will ensure to the best of your ability that the person you select will be seen as a leader by staff and the community alike. In truth, any intelligent person can learn how to establish the library's budget; more important will be someone who has a strong commitment behind the "why"—the priorities the budget represents. Any intelligent person can become an active and valuable player in a building project or a capital campaign; more important will be someone who is excited about the prospect and knows exactly how these efforts will impact library services of the future.

If you are fortunate, you will all leave with an overwhelming consensus that one of the candidates is just the right person to lead the library into the future. On the other hand, there may be serious divergence among the team on who is best. Don't hesitate to bring back the top two contenders.

If no one stands out during the interview process, don't hesitate to start the process over. This may take up to even a year and that's a true morale buster, but just know that if you hire the wrong person because you didn't want to extend a search, you will live with that decision for a lot longer than a year and it will be more painful.

REFERENCES

Abraham Lincoln was right—you can fool all of the people some of the time. As thorough as your process has been, it is possible that someone has pulled the wool over your collective eyes during the interview process. Be sure to follow up when you've selected your top candidate by checking his or her references—including those not listed by the candidate and which may be available by calling past employers.

It is completely legitimate for candidates to tell you that they would rather you didn't check with their board of trustees, city manager, or whomever the boss is until you are ready to make an offer. Sometimes there are repercussions in the workplace when it's discovered that a staff member or current library director is looking for another job. However, if you are ready to make an offer, you must get in touch with the top candidate's supervisor. If he or she balks at this point, you may well be dealing with someone who has something to hide.

In addition to the references listed, it's a good idea to call a workplace from the top candidate's past. If he or she has held more than one job prior to making this application, there is no reason not to contact that place of employment and see what you can find out. It is usually (but not always) the case that those you contact will be thrilled to sing your candidate's praises if he or she was respected and admired. If you get the human resources–approved statement that the former employer can only give out length and dates of employment, you might want to worry. Contacting at least three people for whom your candidate worked is critically important insurance.

Evaluating the Library Director

An important way to ensure and support a highly effective library director is to commit to meaningful performance appraisals at least annually. It's surprising how often this very important duty gets short shrift or even overlooked altogether. Even if you are having problems with your director (perhaps especially if you are having problems with your director), the evaluation process should be a positive and highly productive way of ensuring that your director is meeting his or her goals and that, as a result, the library is moving forward.

Ideally, what is outlined in a performance review should not come as a surprise to anyone involved. This is because the board or its executive committee should have had a discussion at the beginning of each year to set goals for achievement and professional growth with the director. These should be goals that are negotiated with the expected outcomes that clearly state how this will help move the library forward in fulfilling its mission. If you've completed a strategic plan, the goals should be linked to the plan.

By linking evaluation to goal completion, the board can be assured that the director and the board are heading in the same direction and have identified the same priorities. In addition, this link keeps the evaluation as objective as any evaluation can ever be and, therefore, it should be an honest assessment that leads to the groundwork of setting the next year's goals. By negotiating goals for achievement ahead of time, the director and the board know what is expected, thereby avoiding any "gotchas" in the process.

Whatever method you use for evaluating performance, it is critical to do so in writing. The director deserves a written evaluation and a copy should also be placed in his or her personnel file. In addition, if you are in the process of working with a director who is not fully meeting expectations (more on this in the section Coaching a Low-Performing Director on p. 51), these evaluations will be evidence of your expectations and the director's performance—at least as you see it and have articulated it to him or her.

When determining, with the director, what performance goals to focus on for the coming year, a good place to start is with the director's job description (see the section Position Description on p. 39) and the most recent strategic plan. While the board oversees and often initiates the planning process, the director is ultimately responsible for its implementation. Therefore, this is a good document by which to assess where the library is currently and where it needs to go to meet the goals of the plan.

Though not necessarily a comprehensive list of focus areas, generally the library director should be evaluated on these aspects:

- **Staff relationships and management**. If a staff suffers from low morale or a lack of leadership, service delivery will suffer. It's important to assess whether a director is interacting in a positive way with staff. This can be a tricky area for assessment. On the one hand, you do not want to have staff members coming to you to report on negative aspects of a director's performance. This is an area ripe for a disgruntled employee to exact revenge and is a highly dysfunctional course of action. There should, instead, be a written grievance policy and all employees should be compelled to follow it if they have concerns. If you've had several grievances, this should be of concern and should be discussed with the director as soon as possible to try to ascertain the legitimacy of the complaints.

    Many boards struggle with the idea of having the staff evaluate the director. This can help to identify problems if you suspect they are there. In a library where staff is doing excellent work and there are no signs of low morale, however, staff evaluations of the director can end up causing problems where there were none. Again, these evaluations—often done with the promise of anonymity—are perfect tools for gripes of all stripes, whether legitimate or not, and create a situation where the director is, in a way, accountable to staff rather than the other way around.

    It may be that the best way to evaluate this is for board members to look at the overall accomplishments of the director and the staff. If these are high, there is probably a high degree of mutual respect and cooperation in place.

It also helps to talk to the director about the various teams that are in place, what their goals are, and what they've accomplished. Certainly, trustees who visit and use the library should be able to see whether the quality of service is consistently high and friendly—if not, this could be another sign of trouble.

- **Library goals as stated in the strategic plan.** Are efforts ongoing? Is the entire staff engaged? What outcomes are evident from the work of the staff and director that show achievement and continuous improvement? What specific goals have been accomplished and which ones will need added focus in the coming year?

- **Financial responsibility and oversight.** Is the budget on target? Is the money well spent during the course of the year and are the books in the black? Do the programs supported by the budget reflect the priorities set by the board and the strategic plan?

  What about financial development? Does the library director work well with the Friends group and foundation? Have there been efforts to reduce the costs of outside services to the library in order to maximize the collection and programs budgets? Have grants been written? Have partnerships been created with civic organizations to help fund special literacy projects?

- **Overall quality of library services.** How innovative are your library services? Do you get feedback from the public about the quality and scope of the collection? Are your services highly used? What kind of media attention do library services get? Do the services delivered meet or attempt to meet the goal of reaching everyone in the community? How does the director determine the effectiveness of service design and delivery and in what ways does he or she make changes to continuously improve services?

- **Community relations.** Is the library director identifiable as a leader in the community? Does he or she participate in task forces and committees within the community? Is the library regularly highlighted in the media? Does the director have the respect of community government leaders? Does the director foster a library volunteer program? Is he or she a high-profile library promoter?

- **Facilities management.** Does the director ensure that the library is always clean, safe, and well maintained? If the budget for maintenance upkeep is lacking, what has the director done to try to address this issue? Are marketing and merchandising techniques used to highlight the library's collections and services? Is there good signage within the library to help patrons access various areas of service? Are signs directing community members to the library facility clear and visible? Is the exterior of the library inviting?

- **Board relationships.** How well is the director communicating with the board? Is the board kept up to date on all pertinent issues? Does the director take time to discuss national and statewide trends that may have an impact on local services? Do board packets contain meaningful information that helps members conduct their business, understand trends, and set policy?

These are some broad areas for discussion both in setting goals at the beginning of the year and in assessing their accomplishment during the evaluation process. The board should be very careful to stay away from objectives or dictating exactly how the goals should be achieved. Remember, the director is the one with the professional education and experience. He or she will be evaluated on outcomes. If the methods for obtaining those outcomes (assuming they are safe and legal) aren't within the director's authority, it will be unfair to judge him or her on the performance of those outcomes.

The process of evaluation differs with every board. A small board might act as a committee of the whole for evaluating the director. Other boards will delegate this responsibility to its executive committee or a special board task force. All board members should have an opportunity to give input, however, even if not directly involved in the performance evaluation itself. This input should include how well goals have been met, how well the library is doing in its performance measures, and how effective each board member believes the director to be.

Using quantifiable measures of library performance (such as circulation statistics, visits per year, etc.), the perceptions of board members, and the negotiated goal areas from the previous year, the board or its committee has a very good basis for discussion and evaluation.

Coaching a Low-Performing Director

Unfortunately there are some low-performing directors out there. The reasons for this are probably as numerous as the directors themselves. The blame for continued low performance, however, resides squarely on the board of trustees. That's right—it may not be pleasant to think about, but if you are the governing board with full authority for hiring, evaluating, and—if necessary—firing directors, you must take this responsibility extremely seriously. As mentioned before, the library will only ever be as good as its director.

If you have a low-performing director, there is some good news. In many cases, clearer communication of expectations will solve the problem along with regular feedback on performance. This means more than the annual evaluation. If you have a library director who is not living up to your expectations (and these should be objective, based on the position description for director and on your planning and mutually agreed-upon goals for library success), you will need to institute a plan of regular and honest follow-up with the director.

These sessions should be as objective as possible. It would be wonderful if everything about performance could be fact based, but such qualities as good communication (the director could be doing a lot of it but not much that is pertinent or meaningful), community involvement (the director could belong to several outside organizations but never actively participate), or budget management (he or she could be landing in the black every year, but never make any suggestions for changes that would allow new services or creative projects) are not quantifiable. It becomes important, therefore, to discuss any perceived lapses in leadership qualities and it should be stated (in writing) what outcomes would indicate to the trustees that there has been notable improvement.

Each discussion, which should be focused on outcomes expected and low performance outlined, must include a written summary. Keep one file and give one to the director. Coaching is not a job for the faint of heart (or for that one trustee who just doesn't like the director), but it does constitute due diligence. There is every possibility that you can turn this situation around, but that won't happen if you don't have the courage and put in the effort. Failing to communicate with a low-performing director will negatively impact library services and staff. As hard as coaching can be, the next step will be firing the director—something that will be much harder if you haven't done the coaching in the first place.

Firing the Library Director

You may have made a mistake in hiring or you may have inherited a poorly performing library director. It's even possible that the director was once excellent but due to a variety of reasons just isn't performing to expectations any longer. In any case, once you have done the appropriate coaching, evaluating, and discussion of expectations with the director, you may come to the decision to let the director go.

This is a tragedy for everyone involved. The trustees are likely to feel guilty that they can't find another way around this. The director will surely have his or her reputation tarnished and it will be a blow to the director's income and family. This is not easy, but if you've tried to remediate the performance, if you've been very clear about expectations, if you are honest and fair in your evaluations, it is nothing short of your official obligation to dismiss a poorly performing director.

The board is accountable to the public, not the director. The board is ultimately responsible for the quality of library services delivered based on resources available. Given this very important responsibility, you are doing your duty—the right thing—in terminating the director's employment.

In a closed meeting and once the board has decided that this step must be taken (consult your bylaws for what constitutes a majority in this case), the board should let the director know that he or she is being relieved of his or her duties effective immediately. Whatever separation agreement you have determined appropriate should be addressed at this time. The director should have the opportunity to clear out his or her office (have boxes available in advance) and then should leave the premises.

This action is going to have both positive and negative effects on the staff. There will be those who were loyal to the director and those who will give a sigh of relief. But do expect that in any case this will impact the staff and have them worried (perhaps for their own jobs) and talking about this for several weeks to come. It does no one any good to have the director around for any longer than necessary, making this situation worse by his or her presence.

A Note about the Law and Employment Termination

Many states have at-will employment laws under which the director would fall. This means that the director does not have a contract and the employer can fire employees without cause. Even in an at-will situation, however, the director is entitled to certain legal protections. For example, he or she cannot be fired for discriminatory reasons or for reasons that violate the law or public policy.

According to Smith, even in absence of a written contract, there may be an implied contract that will carry weight in litigation:

> Often these cases involve employee personnel manuals, with the employee claiming that the manual or handbook sufficiently established the conditions of employment to permit the court to find that a contract is implied and to bind the parties by the manual's terms and conditions. An employee manual ought to contain a clear disclaimer of any intent to create an employment contract because some courts will recognize and enforce a disclaimer of this kind.[1]

If not at will, your city or state will have laws that prescribe the rules for terminating employees. It's also possible that the director has a contract that stipulates exactly what would be cause for termination and what the consequences for wrongful termination will be. The stated causes for termination may be open to interpretation—the board's and the director's.

Unfortunately, too many library director firings end up in courts of law and/or in the courts of the media. Neither is desirable for either the library or the members of the board. The very best advice is for the board to consult an attorney before taking this final step. Have the attorney look over all performance evaluation documentation, any director responses to those evaluations, and any contracts that exist between the board and the director. An attorney who specializes in employment law or the city's attorney will be your best defense against a suit for wrongful termination.

Do not let the law scare you. If you are in the right and have done due diligence with regard to communicating your concerns with the director, if you have set benchmarks for improvements in the coaching process, and if you can clearly show why the library is suffering at the hands of this director, you must—must—do your job and fire the director whose performance is subpar.

Note

1. Stephen R. Smith, "Directors and Officers on Behalf of the Board," in *The Nonprofit Legal Landscape*, ed. Ober/Kaler (Washington, DC: BoardSource, 2005), 28.

4

Ensuring a Better Future: Strategic Planning

No library can continue to meet changing community needs let alone experience continuous improvement without committing to strategic planning on a regular basis. From setting a vision for the library to articulating its mission, to establishing a set of goals for achieving that mission, the board can and should be involved every step of the way. The board, after all, represents the community the library serves, so who better to play a significant role in defining what those services should be?

Though some people would just as soon avoid the planning process—it does take time and effort—it really can be very exciting. During the planning process, everyone involved has a chance to learn even more about the library, the community in which it operates, and the environment for libraries at the local, state, and national levels. In addition, the planning process allows the participants to imagine library services in a perfect world (visioning), articulate the value and role of the library to the community (mission), and design a blueprint for bringing the library closer to that perfect vision in alignment with the mission (goals). Really, what could be more exciting than that for people who love and support the library?

Getting Started—The Plan to Plan

Before the planning process even begins, there will questions about the process, the timeline for planning, any costs associated with it, and the extent of trustee involvement. Once the board has decided to embark on the planning process, it should ask the director to submit a report that will answer these basic questions and ensure that the process gets off to a good start. Following are points that should be covered in a preliminary report from the library's director.

What Will Be Achieved in the Planning Process?

This might sound a little like putting the cart before the horse—after all, isn't the plan supposed to dictate what will be achieved? Actually, it's a very good idea to understand exactly why you are engaging in this process in the first place. As a board, you may have decided to undergo planning simply because it hasn't been done in awhile and you understand that it's part of your responsibility to initiate this process from time to time.

By stepping back from the notion that planning is inherently good, you might see that your library is lively, well used, and has a wonderful collection and a well-attended variety of programs. Why mess with success, right?

However well your staff is doing in delivering services, it is always helpful to scrutinize what is working as well as what isn't happening to reach out to more of your community that isn't using the library. Also, though the programs may be well attended, they may be only scratching the surface of what's possible and it may be that though well attended, those coming are the same 25 people. Are there ways to create more diversity? Are their underserved or unserved populations out there?

It is a good idea to have the director articulate in what ways the library might expand upon its mission given additional resources or by redistributing the resources you have. By understanding what you hope to achieve, you will have a better idea of how to frame the process and who should be included in the plan's design.

Importantly, the timeline for the process itself should be considered and recommendations should be made. Will it take a year to design the plan? Will this then be a five-year plan? A three-year plan? Without a timeline for the process, it is likely to languish. Without a determination for the length of time the plan will be in place, it will be hard to measure achievement and evaluate success.

What Resources Will Be Needed to Implement a Thorough Planning Process?

There will be costs in terms of staff time—that's a given—but it should be estimated along with an idea of what areas of existing services will be impacted by this use of staff time. Understand that the staff—very likely already working at capacity—will need to be relieved of other duties during this process to make planning time available. Will there be a hiatus in adult programming? Will there be an acceptable lag time for the ordering and processing of important materials that won't get high demand and are not of immediate importance? Will staff meetings become planning meetings only during the process?

In addition to staff time, there may be costs of promotion to engage the community in the process. Refreshments will be necessary for meetings and focus groups (the Friends can help with this). A larger library system with many branches may decide to hire a planning consultant for the process. In this case, an estimate should be provided for this cost along with suggestions for funding it. If the plan will be published, there will be costs attendant to this as well—though serious consideration should be given to electronic-only publishing of the plan.

How much time will be needed by trustees in the process? Will the entire board be involved beyond board meetings? If not, how many board members should be involved and in what ways? The trustees need to understand that they should be engaged in the process—not in implementing it or administrating it, but in providing their own perspective on various committees and task forces.

Overview of Existing Services and Recent Accomplishments

Although, of course, the board should be well versed on both existing services and recent accomplishments, this overview is a good way to bring the information together and if these services and accomplishments are a result of a former planning process, that is good information to have. This inventory may well spark new ideas as the process progresses and it will give those who aren't as familiar with all the library's services a better understanding of what's already in place.

Roles and Responsibilities During the Process

Even though the board often initiates the process, what is their role beyond that? Who will comprise the planning team and what will be their responsibilities? How often will they be expected to meet and how much authority will this team have to hire consultants, develop task forces, and make assignments?

What is the staff's role? Will they write and conduct the surveys? Will they design and bring together various focus groups? Will they be scheduling meetings for various task forces to convene and design goals for various service initiatives? Will they be attaching timelines for achieving the goals and methods for ensuring the outcomes you want? Will they ultimately put the plan together for board approval?

Engaging the Community

Beyond the trustees, who do represent the community at large, there are other groups who should be recruited to participate. These various groups include, for example, the leadership of the Friends group, leaders or staff from other city departments with whom you might partner or who can provide their perspectives during the environmental scan, local government leaders, other civic organization staff members, those who don't currently use the library (if you wish to serve them, you need to find out what they want), and new populations in town such as new ethnic populations, a growing family community, or an aging population.

You won't get a plan that addresses what's missing in your services if you don't reach beyond your current usual suspects. This plan to plan should identify the types of groups that will be included to ensure a very diverse set of perceptions and ideas.

The Environmental Scan

Our world is changing rapidly—there's no doubt about that. You can barely buy a new cell phone that seemingly does everything before the next new edition with even more applications becomes available. You take pride in the fact that your library has something for everyone in the community, and then a new industry opens in your community bringing new Americans, many of whom are just learning English. You install a wonderful (and expensive) state-of-the-art video learning center and a year later, distance learning becomes computer based with Webcams. How on earth can a library reasonably keep up with the changing environment within which it operates?

The truth is, you won't be able to predict the future 100 percent of the time, but you can make reasonable guesses about what trends will have an impact. The plan, after all, won't be dictating what software vendor to choose when your automated catalog needs an update, but it will help illuminate what kinds of applications the system might require based on what changes you anticipate (both in use and in technology) for the future.

Following are descriptions of what an environmental scan should include, followed by ways to gather the information you want and ways to make sense of it.

Your Community

Everyone has a perception about his or her community—it's rural, it's urban, it's poor, it's a wealthy bedroom community to a major metropolitan area. The community is very well educated or heavily composed of blue-collar workers. The community is aging and young families are moving out, or they are moving in. The culture supports and values lifelong learning of all types, or it doesn't and all cultural institutions struggle to engage the community.

The best way to assess your community and its support (or probable support) for your library is to gather both quantitative data and qualitative data. In the environmental scan for assessing the community, you'll want to look at the following:

- **Demographics**. What is the population of your community? What is the breakdown of the population? Has this been stable for a number of years? Are there changes in population density and distribution, age and gender, socioeconomic status, ethnic status? All this information is readily available through census information and through your town's or city's own planning data. It will be important for you to see how the demographics of your community are changing (if they are) because this information will be important as you determine the types of materials and services you'll want to provide in the coming years.

- **The tax issue**. The scan should include an assessment of how your community views the financial support of various institutions—particularly your library. Taxes are a dirty word for many, but the truth is, libraries (and roads, bridges, schools, sewers, parks, etc.) can't live without them. A review of the success or failure of recent tax-based initiatives along with surveys and focus groups will help you figure out whether or not your plan needs a heavy public awareness component or, on the other hand, a stronger programming component to engage those who value community service.

- **Competition**. The community scan should look at the various providers of the same (ostensibly) types of services your library provides—is there a comprehensive Head Start program? Do you have a lot of bookstores and do they offer programs—are they free? Is there a strong writers' community in town? Do they provide author programs open to the public? How about a Reading Is Fundamental (RIF) program available to children in your community—who is providing the service?

In truth, you'll probably find that those services that seem to offer similar programs and services do have fundamental differences, such as that they aren't free; they aren't available to everyone in the community; and/or they have singular agendas and audiences.

There is probably little actual competition from others in your community, but taking an inventory will allow you to either (1) articulate the differences in a public awareness plan, and/or (2) highlight possible partnership opportunities with others who have similar missions.

In addition to making a list of possible competitors in your community, you should use your focus groups to find out if people see them as viable alternatives to library service. By the way, focus groups are not the time to make the case for the library—good focus group results will reveal to you both strengths and weaknesses in your library's services and perceptions about the strengths and weaknesses of your service. It's as important to know what people think about the library, even (especially) if it isn't true. *More on focus groups later.*

Your Library

Though you look at library use statistics quite often, for the environmental scan you'll want to look at how the use of various services is changing. For example, is the book circulation down but computer use up? How are patrons using your public access terminals—for job searches, entertainment, research (including how much they use subscription databases and which ones)? Are the types of books being checked out changing? Is the circulation of how-to books on the decline? Just what information should you be looking at to assess your library?

In addition to use statistics, you should look at a summary of public comments that the library has received over the past several years—in the media, at public library meetings, and through the library's suggestion box or via online comments. While you'll have some good strong quantitative data in use and attendance statistics, a qualitative assessment that can come from those who use the library will be valuable.

Use Statistics

This is a concrete way to see just exactly how much your library is being used and in what ways. You will want to look at the numbers for the following:

- **Circulation.** Is it up or down over the past years? What types of materials are circulating well—children's, DVDs, CDs, biographies, self-help, for example?

- **Library card registration.** How many are registered and what is the age breakdown for registration? Is registration increasing each year? Staying about the same? Declining?

- **Gate count.** How many people come into your library each year? What days and times tend to be the busiest?

- **Program attendance.** How many attend adult programs? How many attend children's? Are these numbers changing over time and in what way?

- **Reference.** How many reference questions are answered each year and when is reference service busiest? What types of questions are being asked? Are the numbers of questions on the decline? On the rise?

- **Computer use.** How many patrons log on to public access computers each year and for how many hours of total use? What are they accessing—job search databases, in-house databases, readers' advisory databases, homework helper databases?

- **Outreach services.** In what ways is the library taking services to those outside of the library's walls and how many are these services reaching?

- **Meeting room use.** How many groups are using your meeting room each year? How many are turned away because of unavailability?

The Public's Perception

While use statistics give you answers as to what services the patrons are using and how much they are using them, it is also very important to find out why they use certain services, what they value most about services, and, importantly, why they are not using the library's services.

The best way to try to get a handle on how the public sees your library and its services is to communicate with them. There are a variety of ways to do this, including the following.

Focus Groups

Focus groups are an excellent way to become a fly on the wall and to hear what people really think about the library. The notion of being a fly on the wall means that you are, basically, invisible. Therefore, it is important that focus groups are led by people not associated with the library. You really want honest answers and discussions within the group. Folks may be reluctant to talk about unfriendly service or unfavorable hours with a library representative in the room.

If your library has the resources, it might be a good idea to hire someone who has experience in leading focus groups. This person will work with the planning team to determine what kinds of information the team hopes to garner from the groups. For example, how aware are users and nonusers of the various services you offer? What services are highly valued? For those in the focus groups of those who don't use the library, why don't they? In what other ways do people get the information and reading materials they need?

An experienced consultant will be able to advise your team on the number and makeup of focus groups that will work best for you. You may be satisfied with one group of both users and nonusers that represents a variety of ages, backgrounds, and ethnicities. On the other hand, you might want to separate groups by users versus nonusers or teens versus adults.

In order to capture the nature of the conversations and to ensure that all opinions go into the record, there should be a second person to take notes and to tape the sessions. This person, along with the group leader, will later listen to the tape and go over the notes to put together an executive summary of what was said to turn in as part of the environmental scan. The notes and tapes themselves should be available throughout the process, but in an effort to avoid information overload, the executive summary will be a welcome and satisfactory report.

SURVEYS

Conducting surveys of your library users and nonusers is a good way to get the opinions of a lot of people in your community. The real effort in conducting a survey should be the design of the survey itself. You want to carefully consider your questions so that they are clear and elicit the information you really want.

Good surveys should be as short as possible so people will take the time to complete them. A survey can include simple yes or no questions, questions that ask people to rate the quality of library services, questions that ask respondents to prioritize services, and questions that require a checkoff response, such as, "How do you learn about library programs?" with sample choices of: the media, in the library, word of mouth, on the radio, flyers posted downtown, at school, etc.

It's also a good idea to include a space in the survey for comments. You may not have asked a question on a topic about which the respondent wishes to comment. Sometimes you can learn the most from a response about something you didn't ask.

The trick with surveys is getting those who don't use the library to fill them out. In this case, there will probably be a second survey designed especially for nonusers. The questions on this survey will ask such questions as, "What are the reasons you don't use the library?" Ask respondents to prioritize such answers as: the library hours don't work for me; I don't have time; I buy my books; I've had unfriendly service there in the past; the library doesn't have anything I want.

In a nonuser survey you can take the opportunity to educate as well. For example, a question such as, "Which of the following did you know the library offers?

(Check all that apply.)" Then you can list ten services you think nonusers might be unaware of. This is both a chance to educate them about what you do have and a chance for you to see which services need more marketing.

In conducting nonuser surveys, the approach for getting responses will need to be a bit more aggressive—if a person doesn't use the library, why would he or she bother to fill out a library survey? Consider asking members of the planning team or Friends group to take nonuser surveys to other organizations that they belong to asking those who seldom or never use the library to fill them out.

Paper surveys are still a good way to get a lot of responses, but they will have to be tabulated, and this can take time. Consider asking your Friends group to set up a task force for the distribution and tabulation of surveys and be sure to make the surveys available at the library.

Another way to survey community members is electronically. This makes it easy to tabulate responses, but the number of responses you get will likely be less unless you are able to get the electronic survey placed on a number of Web sites in addition to the library's site. Look into using such tools as SurveyMonkey.com and other similar online polling services.

You should also tabulate online and suggestion box comments (and/or other avenues you provide on a regular basis for public input).

STATE AND NATIONAL TRENDS AND ISSUES

It's very easy to look no further than your own community when doing the environmental scan, but the truth is that what is happening on the state and national levels can, indeed, impact your library and its services. A good director will keep the board informed of these issues on an ongoing basis, but it's also important to look a little more closely during the planning process. For example, the following are issues beyond your community that have impacted and will impact your library.

STATE

It's important to know what's going on with your state's budget and how this will affect libraries. Even in good times, it's possible that a governor or legislator doesn't see the value in libraries and thinks that cutting funding to the state library—or direct funding to localities—would enable them to focus more money on areas that they believe are more important. And we all know what happens during tough economic times.

Typically, the state library provides funding for interlibrary loan and shared information databases—databases that are important to your library's patrons, but would be cost prohibitive if your library had to purchase them on its own. In addition, the state library provides continuing education opportunities—especially to support staff, and this type of education and training is rarely available elsewhere.

NATIONAL

While your local library does not receive much, if any, direct operational funding from the federal government, it does receive some indirect support via the state library (see previous section), and may receive grants from the Institute of Museum and Library Services (IMLS) and/or through the Library Services and Technology Act (LSTA). In addition, your library may receive e-rate funding that helps offset the costs of telecommunications for qualifying libraries. It's important to know whether these funds are threatened and how they could impact your planning.

Beyond funding, Congress does, from time to time, pass laws that have an impact on your library. For example, the Children's Internet Protection Act (CIPA) essentially requires either (a) filtering of computer terminals used by children, or (b) forfeiture of government e-rate funds. Both have philosophical as well as financial consequences for your library.

Though the board should be informed about national issues that affect the library throughout the year, during this planning process it is especially important to see what, if anything, is coming down the pike that could change your plans once in place.

Creating the Future: The Strategic Plan

Because the board is charged with oversight and guidance of the overall direction the library takes in determining and delivering services, they should be involved in brainstorming the library's vision and mission statement. In addition, along with library administrative staff, they should be involved in coming up with three to four strategic areas for the plan to address (goals). Once this has been decided, the staff will work to design and implement strategies to meet the goals and that are in keeping with the overall vision and mission of the library.

The Vision

The environmental scan should be a very illuminating process but once it is complete, it's time to start thinking of what your library would look like in a perfect world, and then design a plan that will bring you closer to this dream. This is the really fun part.

During the visioning session, you describe the library and its services in the future. What would you like your library to look like in five years? Forget about budgetary constraints, space limitations, and unfriendly political climates. For a moment, think about your library as it would be if it were perfect. As you work through this process, you will create a vision that is ultimately realistic and achievable, but why not start from the top?

Yours should be a shared vision. Using the feedback from the focus groups and surveys, begin to assess how your community sees the library and what your community would like for library services. This is a good time for the entire board to be involved along with the staff. Working on a vision statement together will be a wonderful kickoff to the work of the plan itself. While not everyone involved will agree on the vision, as many people as possible should have a chance to share theirs.

Once the ideas and thoughts have coalesced and condensed, the planning team or the board along with the library's director can work on a vision statement that captures the collective dream. The following are a few vision statements that do this:

- The Park Ridge Public Library will be a gathering place where all citizens are welcome to pursue their interests, expand their ideas, learn new skills, interact with other members of the community, and enhance their quality of life. (Park Ridge, Illinois)

- A world of information and ideas within reach of every Calgarian. (Calgary, Canada)

- Our community will discover library resources and programs that anticipate and satisfy their needs for everyday information, enjoyment, and enlightenment.

  Our community will look to the library for accurate, thorough answers to their questions, guided by friendly, knowledgeable staff.

  Our community will have library resources to support schoolwork and independent learning at every age, helping to build skills and interests needed for lifelong success.

  Champaign's children will grow up in an environment that is rich in stories and literature, where reading is valued and encouraged.

  Our community will be drawn to welcoming, safe library environments that reflect the community's changing needs. (Champaign, Illinois)

As you can see from the previous examples, the vision statement reflects the best of all possible worlds for these libraries in their community. These statements can range from the specific (Park Ridge, Illinois), to the lofty (Calgary, Canada), to the comprehensive (Champaign, Illinois).

The Mission

The mission statement is important because it articulates in just a few sentences the library's role in the community. A good mission statement can and should be used in marketing materials, in the newsletter's front-page banner, and on the library's Web site to inform everyone about the role and the values of the library. The mission statement should inform the goals of the planning process and justify all of the library's services.

In truth, the mission of the public library has not changed radically over the years. You may find that yours is still an effective and complete statement of purpose. Because the mission statement can and should be widely shared, you might want to at least tweak it so that it is succinct and memorable:

- The mission of the Sharon Public Library is to serve the informational, educational, cultural, and recreational needs of all members of the Sharon community by providing access to a professional staff, a state-of-the-art facility, and quality materials, programs, and services. (Sharon, Massachusetts)

- Libraries were established to provide information to all who inquire. Librarians are dedicated to gathering, organizing, and disseminating the world's knowledge. No matter the format, be it print, media, microform, or electronic, the Glen Cove Public Library supports freedom of access to the broadest spectrum of ideas. For many users, the library is the last line of defense in the search for truth. (Glen Cove, New York)

- The El Paso Public Library serves our diverse community through information access, cultural enrichment, and lifelong learning. (El Paso, Texas)

With these three examples, it's easy to see that mission statements can range from those that include qualities such as "state-of-the-art" and "professional staff" (Sharon, Massachusetts), to the beautifully lofty (Glen Cove, New York), to the short and succinct (El Paso, Texas). What they all have in common, however, is that they emphasize their roles—education, culture, information, recreation—and they emphasize that their services are available to everyone in the community.

The Goals

Setting goals will begin to create the blueprint for achieving the library's vision and mission. Going back to the materials collected in the environmental scan, the planning team should begin to think about both its existing services and those that might be new and innovative. In addition, information from the surveys and focus groups might reveal that some services should be changed or improved to meet community needs.

Since goals reflect the big picture for accomplishment, they will state in broad terms what the library will work toward during the next three to five years. Because you want the plan to be both realistic and achievable, it makes sense to limit your plan to three to five goal areas. During the environmental scan, you may, for example, note that the following key issues have emerged:

- Many new Spanish-speaking families are moving into the community.

- Many people aren't able to get to your library when it's open.

- There is a perception that the public service staff members are not friendly and helpful.

- More people are accessing the library remotely from their home or offices.

This kind of information could well form the basis for your goals. The following are examples of goal areas that are designed to respond to the previous issues discovered in the environmental scan:

- The library will provide a comprehensive collection of materials in various formats, along with programs and outreach services to accommodate all the diverse needs of our changing community. This goal area is designed to ensure that all the library's resources are available to everyone regardless of ethnicity, native language, or preferred format. It doesn't specifically address Spanish-speaking citizens but is broader to include all those who in former years might have been described as nontraditional library users.

- The library will develop a service schedule to maximize access by everyone both on site and remotely. While not specifically dictating that the library increase or change its open hours of operation, it does focus on the need to do the best so that everyone can get to the facility and it also takes into account that, increasingly, people are using their library's services remotely.

- The library will provide courteous, professional, and excellent service to every single library patron every time they use the library. Whether by workshops, firings, and/or personal coaching, the end result will be that every single person who walks into the library will be greeted by a welcoming staff. Certainly a goal for every library.

- The library will provide a variety of services that will enhance the library experience of remote users. This goal comes from the findings in the environmental scan that showed that more and more people wish to download books, do research, and ask reference questions from their home or office.

Once the plan, including the goals, has been completed, the board need only approve it and ensure that regular progress is being made in its attainment. No strategies for accomplishing these goals are listed because (a) this is an area to be left strictly to staff, and (b) strategies should be as flexible as possible. Never before has the library's environment been so volatile. The goals remain consistent, but methods for achieving them will no doubt change over time.

Measuring Success

Setting goals without providing some criteria for evaluation would be like sending all your good work and intentions down a black hole. How will you know if what you've designed is being implemented and is working? It's important that the board ask the director to give an update report on the plan's progress regularly and that the update includes impacts.

To measure the results of your efforts, you can use many of the same tools you did during the environmental scan. Watching such trends as circulation, library visits, and computer use will show if you've made some good strides in increasing use. As with the environmental scan, however, some of the qualitative improvements will best be determined through surveys, comment boxes, and even focus groups reconvened after a year or two of the plan implementation.

At the end of the planning cycle (three to five years), you will have the satisfaction of seeing how your hard work has paid off to ensure that the library is, indeed, meeting the needs of the community. Now it is time to take a new look at your environment, look at the vision and mission statements you developed, and set some new goals for continuous improvement of your library's services.

5

An Essential Role: Developing and Approving Policies

An important role for the board of trustees is to ensure that there is a set of policies in place that will guide the practice and decision making of library staff and ensure the rights and responsibilities of library users. Fundamentally, good library policies will ensure that library users are treated equitably and within a framework that best meets the needs of community members and maximizes the library's resources for the shared use of all patrons.

Another set of policies will govern the treatment of library staff members. If the library is a department of the town, city, or county where it is located, it could well be that all personnel policies come from the municipality's human resources department. They will include policies for hiring and termination, grievance procedures, benefits, and so on. If your library is a separate entity from the city or county, you will develop your own policies. It will be helpful to look at the municipality's personnel policies as a model for developing your own. Equitable treatment of library staff with other city employees is important for maintaining goodwill on the part of the library staff and the city's staff.

While the director may initially draft policies (or draft updates of existing policies), the trustees will ultimately have to stand behind them. For this reason, each board member should understand clearly the underlying purpose for each policy, understand how it is implemented, and read any new, proposed, or updated policies very carefully.

When considering a new policy or an update, the director should provide a rationale along with the draft or update to the board members at least two weeks prior to the meeting where the policy will be discussed. Even though governing boards have the legal responsibility and authority to make policy, the quality and effectiveness of the policies usually depends on the staff who have the experience to understand the impacts of various policies (good and bad) and can research options and prepare drafts.

Creating and Approving Excellent Policies

A good policy will begin with a statement of purpose. Why does the library enforce this policy? What is the reasoning behind it? A good statement of purpose will help those who might challenge a policy better understand why it exists in the first place. In addition, it will underline the library's value for equitable access and ease of use by all patrons. All policies should be contained in a single manual and all should be easily available to the public, both online and in hard copy.

It is often easier to create new policies or benchmark your existing policies when you have samples of what other libraries are doing. The following are sample policies selected from libraries of all sizes across the country that are particularly good models. Of course, they won't always meet your particular requirements, but they can provide you with a framework for discussion.

- **Materials selection and collection development policy**. This is usually the most complex and important policy in the library. This policy controls the heart of your services—your collection. A collection development policy should cover all types of materials and it should include a "request for reconsideration of material(s)" form. Figure 5.1 is the collection development policy from the Ames Public Library in Iowa, which is very clear and comprehensive. Figure 5.2 is a sample "Request for Reconsideration of Library Resources" from the Office of Intellectual Freedom of the American Library Association.

- **Meeting room policy**. Meeting rooms are an important library resource in every community and there is often a lot of competition for their use. A good policy that outlines the rules and limitations of meeting room use along with considerations for determining priority of use will help ensure that this limited resource is maximized for the public it serves. Figure 5.3 is a good example of a meeting room policy that thoroughly explains not only the policy but the rationale behind its prescriptions, from the San Bernardino Public Library in California.

- **Confidentiality of patron records**. Most if not all states have laws to govern and protect patron privacy. It is imperative for intellectual freedom that patrons know that their records are protected. This is a fundamental library policy. Figure 5.4 is a sample from the Hancock Public Library in Indiana and a good example of a short and to-the-point policy that protects patrons' rights.

- **Internet use policy**. The Internet has caused quite a stir in the library world. This is understandable since worlds of information are available to virtually anyone and at any time. Mostly, this is a great thing. However, there has been concern about what children may have access to in the library. Some libraries—those that qualify for and receive e-rate funds—are

---

Figure 5.1. Library Board Policy, Ames Public Library (Ames, IA)

Ames Public Library Policy Board
Section: Library Resource
Subject: Collections
Approved: 11/05
Reviewed:
Revised: 10/08

Policy

Ames Public Library offers collections to further the Library's mission: Ames Public Library—We connect you to the world of ideas. The freedom to know is the foundation of our democracy. Ames Public Library strives to be an information center for the Ames community to preserve and encourage the free expression of ideas essential to informed citizens. The Ames Public Library Board of Trustees has adopted this Collections Policy to provide guidance for the selection and evaluation of materials to anticipate and meet the needs of the Ames community.

Responsibility for selection

The Ames Public Library Board of Trustees delegates authority for the selection of materials to the Library Director and those staff designated by the director as collection managers. The collection managers meet the goals of the Collection Development Policy, oversee the selection process, and provide professional support for materials selectors.

Materials budget

The Ames Public Library Board of Trustees develops an annual materials budget in consultation with the Director. This budget is certified by the Ames City Council. Each year the Collection Managers develop budgets for their selection areas based on factors such as circulation statistics, cost per item, annual collection goals, and support of the strategic plan.

Selection guidelines and practices

The Ames community includes people from diverse educational, cultural and economic backgrounds who display a variety of interests, needs, values and viewpoints. Librarians at Ames Public Library make selections based on an interest and general knowledge of the subject area and its literature, familiarity with the materials in the collection, an awareness of the selection tools for the subject, and recognition of community needs as identified by demographic circulation and other statistical analysis. The librarians apply professional standards and work within specific selection and review procedures.

Selectors recognize the importance of informed citizens who are familiar with their heritage and with issues facing the community. Ames Public Library's strategic plan asserts the following primary goal for collections: Library customers will find materials to stimulate their imagination and enhance their leisure time. Librarians support the role of a popular materials center by selecting materials to serve the full range of ages, cultures, lifestyles, education, and reading skills of citizens. The materials selected reflect the complex culture shared by the community. The collection includes diverse points of view and a choice of formats, treatments, and levels of difficulty. Librarians achieve a balanced collection through the diversity of materials, not an equality of numbers, working within constraints of budgets, availability, and space.

Ames Public Library is a popular materials center and does not attempt to duplicate the research resources of Iowa State University. The library does not collect material to support local curricula except when these materials also serve the general public. The Library does collect supplementary materials

(Continued)

Figure 5.1. Library Board Policy, Ames Public Library (Ames, IA) *(Continued)*

that promote lifelong learning and provide a beginning point for those seeking more advanced information or materials. The collection is generally not archival, and items are expected to be used frequently. The collection managers oversee an annual assessment to ensure that the collection meets current needs and that a substantial percentage of the materials are less than five years old.

Multiple copies

The Ames Public Library responds directly to community and customer interests by purchasing multiple copies. While the Library's budgetary resources do not allow for the purchase of multiple copies for every title owned, the budget is structured to provide multiple copies for high demand items. The number of duplicate copies purchased may be determined by the number of holds for a given type of material. The Library strives to meet temporary demand and still build a collection with breadth and depth.

Formats

Materials are purchased in the most appropriate format for library use. Books are generally purchased in hardcover editions because of their durability; however, if the hardcover is prohibitively expensive, paperback editions are preferred if the title would be used infrequently or is ephemeral.

Ames Public Library recognizes the place of non-print formats in the collection as legitimate educational and recreational resources for the community. The Library monitors the development of new formats and may add these to the collection. The continuation of current formats and the adoption of new formats will be based on an analysis of market acceptance of the format, its ability to provide a cost-effective alternative to existing formats, and the Library's financial ability to acquire, process, and maintain a sufficient collection.

Ames Public Library acquires materials in formats that are useful for citizens with disabilities. Collection managers will develop these collections as demand indicates, and will be alert for new formats that may be appropriate.

World language materials

The Library generally does not acquire materials in languages other than English; nor does it acquire foreign language films that do not provide an option for English subtitles. The Library does maintain a small collection of Spanish language materials of popular fiction and nonfiction in both the adult and youth collections for recreational reading and for those learning the language. Materials in other languages will be added to the extent that interest, space, budget, and cataloging resources allow.

Placement of materials

Ames Public Library catalogers use the Dewey Decimal Classification system and Library of Congress subject headings to place materials in the proper subject area and to assign them to shelving categories. Librarians take into account age recommendations in reviews as they choose and classify materials.

Ames Public Library shelving areas are divided in sections such as Juvenile, Reference, Fiction, and DVDs for ease of use, but customers of any age may use materials in all sections of the library. It is the responsibility of parents or legal guardians, not Ames Public Library staff, to monitor library use by minors.

Interlibrary loan

Interlibrary loan is a transaction in which Ames Public Library borrows materials directly from another library on behalf of its customer, or another library borrows materials from Ames Public Library on

(Continued)

> ## Figure 5.1. Library Board Policy, Ames Public Library (Ames, IA) *(Continued)*
>
> behalf of its customer. Interlibrary loan is not a substitute for collection development. It supports the mission of Ames Public Library by expanding the range of materials available to library customers without needlessly duplicating the resources of other libraries. In meeting customer needs, Ames Public Library follows state and national interlibrary loan protocols. Items in frequent or recurring demand are considered for purchase.
>
> ### Exclusions from collections
>
> Ames Public Library does not keep, acquire or purchase material that violates the legal definition of obscene material as defined by state statute.
>
> No material will be excluded from selection because of the race, ancestry, place of origin, color, ethnic origin, citizenship, creed, sex, sexual orientation, gender identity, age, marital status, receipt of public assistance, political affiliation, disability, educational background and/or socio-economic status of the creator of the work.
>
> Ames Public Library generally does not buy items of a promotional nature, such as those advertised in infomercials.
>
> ### Selection aids
>
> Ames Public Library selectors work under the guidance of collection managers who have the education, training and work experience required to make important selection decisions. They select materials for the Ames Public Library collection by applying statistical data and their knowledge of customer information needs; regional, state and college library collections; publishing industry trends; and the general history of knowledge.
>
> Ames Public Library selectors rely on professional tools for selection. These may include but are not limited to: Booklist, Library Journal, Publisher's Weekly, New York Times Book Review, VOYA, School Library Journal, Horn Book, local newspapers, websites and award winning lists.
>
> Ames Public Library customers are encouraged to recommend purchase of library materials. These requests are evaluated using the selection criteria reflected elsewhere in this policy. "Customer Request Forms" are available at all public service desks, or customers may send an email through our "Ask a Librarian" service on Ames Public Library's website: www.amespubliclibrary.org.
>
> ### Online databases criteria
>
> Materials in electronic format are evaluated using the following criteria:
>
> - Content fits within the mission of Ames Public Library.
> - Provides added value over other formats.
> - Search interface is user-friendly.
> - Available by both remote and in-house access.
> - Unlimited access when possible.
> - Available 24 hours per day, seven days per week.
> - Customer access based on library card number.
> - Vendor provides usage statistics.
> - Reasonable cost.
> - Can be maintained over a variety of computer platforms.
> - Strategic plan priorities.
>
> Ames Public Library will not maintain more than one version of a resource (such as electronic or print) unless there are compelling reasons to do so. Collection managers will conduct an annual evaluation
>
> *(Continued)*

Figure 5.1. Library Board Policy, Ames Public Library (Ames, IA) (Continued)

of electronic materials based on usage statistics. Collection managers will solicit customer feedback when evaluating new products.

Special collections

Ames Public Library supports the acquisition and preservation of useful and important historical, municipal, public school, and genealogical materials relating to Ames and Story County. Materials will be obtained in print and electronic formats. The development of special collections will focus on the following areas:

- **Farwell Brown Photographic Archive**: Ames Public Library will maintain both print and digitized versions of this unique and invaluable archive of local photographs. Ames Public Library will work in cooperation with the Ames Historical Society to develop and maintain the archive.
- **Iowa Room**: Ames Public Library will acquire and maintain useful and important historical and municipal publications relating to Ames and Story County. With the exception of the Farwell T. Brown Photographic Archive and a selected number of videos and DVDs of local historical subjects and municipal meetings, the Iowa Room collection will be limited to publications. Realia and primary print sources will not be collected but will be given to the Ames Historical Society. Ames Public Library will work in cooperation with the Ames Historical Society to determine the disposition of materials of local historical interest and to determine the future direction of the collections in the Iowa Room and at the Ames Historical Society.
- **Genealogy Collection**: Ames Public Library will acquire and maintain relevant genealogical materials in cooperation with the Story County Chapter of the Iowa Genealogical Society. The chapter is responsible for selecting new materials for the genealogy collection.

Collection assessment

Circulating collections undergo an annual assessment to make space for current materials, to make collections more attractive, to facilitate ease of use by customers and staff, and to reduce the damage to materials caused by overcrowding, space limitations, and overuse. Assessment decisions are based on the following criteria:

- Currency
- Accuracy
- Use and vitality based on analysis of collection measures

- Wear and damage
- Durability
- Changes in format
- Duplicated holdings with low demand

- Space limitations
- Community interest
- Availability from other libraries
- Strategic plan priorities

Expressions of concern

Ames Public Library recognizes that some materials are controversial. Any item may offend some customers. Ames Public Library's role is to provide materials which will allow individuals to freely examine subjects and make their own decisions. While customers are free to reject for themselves materials that they do not approve of, they cannot exercise this right of censorship to restrict the freedom of access to others. Selection of materials for the collection is based on the principles described in this policy rather than on the basis of anticipated approval or disapproval.

Selection of any item does not constitute endorsement of the author's viewpoint nor does Ames Public Library endorse particular beliefs or views represented in the collection.

Ames Public Library materials will not be marked or identified to show approval or disapproval of their contents, and no library materials will be sequestered, except to protect them from damage or theft.

(Continued)

Figure 5.1. Library Board Policy, Ames Public Library (Ames, IA) *(Continued)*

Responsibility for reading, listening and viewing of materials by minors rests with their parents or legal guardians. At no time will Ames Public Library staff act *in loco parentis* (in place of the parent). Selection of library materials will not be inhibited by the possibility that they may be read or viewed by children. Parents are encouraged to accompany their children to the library to choose materials.

The Ames Public Library Director and the Board of Trustees are aware that customers may take issue with the inclusion of any specific item in the collection and they welcome the expression of concern by our customers. Customer concerns will be dealt with promptly and courteously as detailed in the following process:

1. Ames Public Library staff will listen to the concern and direct customers to the appropriate collection manager for the material in question (e.g., the Adult, Media, Periodicals, Reference or Youth Collection Manager).
2. The collection manager will discuss the concern with the concerned individual or group. After discussion with the collection manager, a customer who requests further action will complete a "Statement of Concern about Library Resources" form, which will be submitted to the Director.
3. The Director will contact the customer and schedule an appointment to discuss the completed "Statement of Concern about Library Resources" form.
4. After discussion with the Ames Public Library Director, an individual or group still seeking further action will have their "Statement of Concern about Library Resources" form considered by the Ames Public Library Board of Trustees at a regular meeting.
5. At the meeting, the individual or group may present comments following the procedures outlined in the Ames Public Library "Public Participation" policy.
6. The Ames Public Library Director will present a response.
7. The Ames Public Library Board of Trustees will make a final ruling on the concern and send a prompt written response to the individual or group.

References

This policy has been developed in concert with the following Ames Public Library policies and American Library Association Guidance Documents: "Mission Statement," "Gifts," "Internet Use Policy and Guidelines," "Diversity in Collection Development," "Library Bill of Rights," "Materials Selection Policy General Guidelines," "Labels and Rating Systems," "Freedom to Read Statement," "Freedom to View Statement," "Free Access to Libraries for Minors," "Restricted Access to Library Materials," and "Expurgation of Library Materials."

---

also required to place filters on their public access terminals. Figure 5.5 contains a policy from the Hennepin County Library System in Minneapolis, Minnesota, which requires that parents or guardians take the responsibility for their children's access.

Note: This policy does not outline directions about signing up or time limits on usage. These are procedural issues that are best left out of policies because (a) they should be determined by management, and (b) they should be able to flex as often as demand or situations require—policies do not and should not have the same degree of flexibility.

- **Circulation of library materials.** The entire concept for a public library revolves around the notion of a shared set of resources. As early as 1731,

Figure 5.2. Sample Request for Reconsideration of Library Resources

Request for Reconsideration of Library Resources

[This is where you identify who in your own structure has authorized use of this form—director, board of trustees, board of education, etc.—and to whom to return the form.]

Example: The school board of Mainstream County, U.S.A., has delegated the responsibility for selection and evaluation of library/educational resources to the school library media specialist/curriculum committee, and has established reconsideration procedures to address concerns about those resources. Completion of this form is the first step in those procedures. If you wish to request reconsideration of school or library resources, please return the completed form to the Coordinator of Library Media Resources, Mainstream School Dist., 1 Mainstream Plaza, Anytown, U.S.A.

Name: _____ Date: _____

Street Address: _____

City: _____

State: _____ Zip: _____

Phone: _____

Do you represent self? _____ Organization? _____

1. Resource on which you are commenting:

    _____ Book _____ Textbook _____ Video _____ Display _____ Magazine

    _____ Library Program _____ Audio Recording _____ Newspaper

    _____ Electronic Information/Network (please specify): _____

    Other: _____

    Title: _____

    Author/Producer: _____

2. What brought this resource to your attention? _____

3. Have you examined the entire resource? _____ Yes _____ No

4. What concerns you about the resource? (use other side or additional pages if necessary)

    _____

    _____

    _____

5. Are there resources you suggest to provide additional information and/or other viewpoints on this topic? (use other side or additional pages if necessary)

    _____

    _____

    _____

**Figure 5.3. Meeting Spaces Policy, San Bernardino Public Library
(San Bernardino, CA)**

San Bernardino Public Library
Meeting Spaces Policy Statement

PURPOSE

The purpose of the Library meeting spaces is to provide facilities for educational and cultural activities that are part of the library program. The meeting spaces may be used by community groups or organizations that are educational or cultural, provided the groups are non-profit, non-partisan and non-sectarian.

As a general policy, the Library Board declines to provide meeting spaces for sessions conducted by governmental bodies as part of their mandated responsibilities. For example, sessions of the Small Claims Courts would not be welcomed, nor public bankruptcy hearings. The Library Board believes these institutions have a responsibility to provide such physical facilities for themselves, and provision of meeting space in the Library lies outside the basic purpose for which the Library was funded. Commission advisory boards and the like are required to look toward their parent organization for meeting space.

The Library Board has declined to serve as a classroom facility for non-profit institutions because classes require a regular and long-term commitment of space where the first priority has been given to intermittent use by the greatest number of groups possible. Secondly, the Library Board believes those institutions interested in providing classes have a responsibility to provide facilities that lie outside the basic purpose for which the Library is funded. Finally, where class participation requires the payment of fees (whether for payment of the instructor, materials or general registration), one of the basic stipulations governing use of the meeting rooms is that all meetings conducted must be open without charge to the general public. Exceptions to this policy are classes in library science or classes co-sponsored by the Library on subjects for which the Library itself would conduct classes were sufficient staff available (i.e., sign language classes).

The following conditions govern the use of the meeting spaces:

1. **OPEN MEETINGS**: All meetings must be free and open to the public. Seating capacity varies from 10 to 200.

2. **PERMITS**: Application for use of the spaces shall be made in the Administration Office by an adult person representing the group. The permit is not transferable as to group or date. The person who signs the permit assumes the responsibility for the conduct of the group and for any damage to library property and must be present at the meeting.

3. **ADMISSION FEES**: Groups using facilities may not charge admission nor collect money, except for regular dues which do not constitute a charge for admission. This prohibition also applies to advance sale tickets or ticket sales held off the premises of the Library. No sales of any kind may be held in any of the Libraries (including the cost of materials which may be used for instructional purpose). The sole exception to this provision is those sales which are sponsored on behalf of the Library and under its co-sponsorship.

4. **RESERVATIONS**: The room may not be requested for a long series of meeting dates; each meeting must be requested individually.

5. **PREEMPTIVE AUTHORITY**: The Library reserves the right to ask a group to relinquish the meeting room if it is needed for a Library function.

(Continued)

Figure 5.3. Meeting Spaces Policy, San Bernardino Public Library
(San Bernardino, CA) *(Continued)*

6. <u>**PARKING LIMITATIONS**</u>: Space permitting, the Library parking lot is available for a maximum of **two hours** to groups using the meeting rooms. The person who signs the permit is responsible for notifying his group of the parking lot limitations. The lot does not fall under the jurisdiction of the Library, and no parking extensions can be granted nor can parking violations be waived by Library personnel.

7. <u>**ENDORSEMENTS**</u>: Granting of permission to use the room in no way constitutes endorsement of the policies or beliefs of the group by the Library, Library Board of Trustees and the Library Director.

8. <u>**USE OF ALCOHOL**</u>: No alcoholic beverages are permitted in the Library.

9. <u>**SMOKING**</u>: Smoking is prohibited in the public areas of the Library, including lobby, atrium, meeting rooms and restroom.

10. <u>**PARTITIONS**</u>: Groups needing the partition between the two Mary Belle Kellogg rooms must request it in advance. Under no circumstances may any member of the group attempt to move the partition because major damage could result. Groups will be billed for damage.

11. <u>**MEETING DURING REGULAR HOURS OF SERVICE**</u>: Persons attending scheduled meetings at Feldheym must meet during normal hours of service. Persons conducting or attending meetings may not enter the Library until the regular opening time.

12. <u>**MEETING OUTSIDE REGULAR HOURS OF SERVICE**</u>: Any other use outside regular hours will only be allowed upon written request. The security system, fire alarms, locks and cooling controls at Feldheym Central Library require the presence of a security officer. Groups whose meeting times fall outside normal library hours must commit to pay the cost of this service and utilities only outside normal hours.

13. <u>**CANCELLATIONS**</u>: If meeting room reservations are cancelled or changed, the group must inform the Administration Office at Feldheym Central Library. This information is crucial for keeping the use of the community rooms up-to-date. All fees must be prepaid prior to event and are not refundable.

14. <u>**SET UP AND CLEANUP**</u>: THE LIBRARY PROVIDES NO CUSTODIAL SERVICES FOR ORGANIZATIONS USING MEETING SPACES. Setup and cleanup are the responsibility of the groups using the facility (including arrangement of tables and chairs). At the end of the meeting, trash and debris must be bagged and removed to the Library's dumpster at the rear of the building. Fastening or taping any materials to the walls of rooms destroys the finish on the walls. Users will be assessed $50 if they have fastened anything to the walls or painted surfaces of meeting rooms. It is expected the room will be left in the same condition in which it was found. Emergency cleaning will be charged back at cost. Offenders risk revocation of their privilege for future use.

15. <u>**DAMAGE**</u>: Users will be liable for any damage to equipment or facility.

16. <u>**PREPARATION TIME**</u>: The heavy demand for the rooms requires the group to assemble no earlier than the time for which the room is reserved. ALLOW TIME NEEDED FOR SETUP, CLEAN UP, AND FOR RELATED SUPPORT SERVICES SUCH AS CATERERS, PIANO TUNERS AND OTHERS WHEN SCHEDULING THE ROOMS. This time must also be scheduled through the Administration Office.

(Continued)

> ## Figure 5.3. Meeting Spaces Policy, San Bernardino Public Library (San Bernardino, CA) *(Continued)*

17. **REFRESHMENTS**: Special permission must be secured for the serving of a meal and/or light refreshments. (See application form for fee amount.) Containers and utensils are to be provided by the group. Refreshments may be served only in the Mary Belle Kellogg Meeting Rooms and atrium at Feldheym and at Villaseñor's meeting room.

18. **EQUIPMENT**: Your need for the following equipment must be clearly defined on your application: chairs, tables, chalkboard, pianos, rostrums, etc. A public address system is available in the Lecture Hall upon request. It is not appropriate to remove equipment from other meeting areas in the Library for your use when you arrive because the equipment may already be committed to another group by prior reservation. Should a conflict arise the decision of the senior library staff member on duty (or the security guard after normal library hours) will be binding.

    The Library also provides free wireless service throughout the four libraries. A portable public address system, and a DVD/Video large screen projector are available for a fee which is payable at the time of reservation. Audiovisual equipment is subject to availability and requires reservation with the Administration Department at least 48 hours before your program. ALL equipment is used at your own risk and the Library assumes no responsibility in the event of injury to members of your group or responsibility for any breakage or loss that may occur to the equipment while it is in your care.

    Individuals may use the pianos available in our meeting rooms by filling out an 'Application for use of meeting room' prior to the use of a piano. While rooms may be reserved for piano usage up to two weeks in advance, priority will be given to group usage of the meeting room facilities. In addition, the piano in Kellogg Room A may not be used while a meeting is in progress in Kellogg Room B.

19. **STORAGE**: The Library does not have the facilities to store support equipment, supplies or refreshments on a meeting to meeting basis. The Library assumes no liability for the property of those conducting or attending meetings, nor for art or other items being exhibited in the rooms.

20. **COURTESY**: Please remember your group is enjoying a unique privilege in sharing meeting space within a public library. Your organization's consideration for the rights of library patrons is expected.

21. **ROOM CAPACITY**: The Bing Wong Auditorium has a stage and 200 fixed theater seats. According to the California Fire Code, 2001 Edition, Article 25 and Appendex VI-E (Table 10A); the occupant load is 266.
    - *Additional seating: 66*
    - **Rear** (area behind fixed seating): 3 rows at 17 = 51 chairs. Begin placement 2 feet from seat back of last row. Shall not exceed 3 rows @ 17 chairs each. 2 feet provided between rows.
    - **Front** (area across front row of fixed seating): 1 row @ 15 = 15 chairs.
    - Begin placement 2 feet from front row (seat up position). Shall not exceed 1 row @ 15 chairs.
    - Mary Belle Kellogg Multi-purpose Room: 50 per room, 100 per both rooms (partition open).
    - California Fire Code: occupant load is 56 each room, 116 per both rooms.
    - A request for additional seating must be submitted prior to the meeting.

22. **Deposition/Court Reporting**: At its February 2003 Board meeting the Library Board of Trustees approved the use of the small conference rooms for depositions. The fee is $25.

23. The Library Board of Trustees reserves the right to grant exceptions for the good of the Library.

11/8/99, revised 2/07/03, 2/13/03, 9/11/08

Figure 5.4. Confidentiality of Library Records Policy, Hancock Public Library (Greenfield, IN)

Hancock Public Library
900 W McKenzie Rd, Greenfield, IN
(317) 462-5141

Policy on Confidentiality of Library Records

1. The Board of Trustees of the Hancock County Public Library specifically recognizes its circulation records and other records identifying the name of library users to be confidential in nature, in accordance with provisions in the Indiana Code, IC 5-14-3-4 Version a.

2. Further, the Board subscribes to the American Library Code of Ethics, which says in part that "We protect each library user's right to privacy and confidentiality with respect to information sought or received and resources consulted, borrowed, acquired or transmitted."

3. All library employees are advised that such records shall not be made available to any agency of state, federal, or local government except pursuant to such process, order, or subpoena as may be authorized under the authority of, and pursuant to, federal, state, or local law relating to civil, criminal, or administrative discovery procedures or legislative investigative power.

4. Upon receipt of such process, order, or subpoena, the library's officers will consult with their legal counsel to determine if such process, order, or subpoena is in proper form and if there is a showing of good cause for its issuance; if the process, order, or subpoena is not in proper form or if good cause has not been shown, they will insist that such defects be cured.

Based on recommendations of the American Library Association. Adopted by the ALA Council June 28, 1995. See ALA Code of Ethics Appendix A.

Benjamin Franklin realized that everyone in the community would be enriched if those with private libraries donated them for public use. He created The Library Company, which is still in existence today. With opening of The Library Company, the idea for sharing a commonly held collection for the use and benefit of all was born.

Today we follow the same model—though rather than donations of private libraries we now receive public monies for what we now consider an essential public service. In order to ensure that everyone has access to the materials of the library, it is essential that the concept of sharing be codified, which is why libraries all have circulation policies.

The circulation policy of the Oliver Wolcott Library in Litchfield, Connecticut, is framed with the American Library Association's Library Bill of Rights and Freedom to Read Statement to emphasize their commitment to free and equal access to library materials (Figure 5.6). It also includes a "no fines" statement—rather, the encouragement to return materials comes from the suspension of library privileges after a specified period of time.

- **Acceptable conduct policy.** As a public facility, it is incumbent upon trustees to set policy that helps to keep the library safe and welcoming for all. Though these policies are typically called acceptable conduct or acceptable

---

Figure 5.5. Library Board Policy, Hennepin County Library (Minneapolis, MN)

Hennepin County Library Board Policy
Internet Use Public Policy
Section: LB12
Tracking Record:
Date Approved: 02/28/07
Previous Policy Dated: 05/24/06
Review Date: Spring 2010

Hennepin County Library provides public access to the Internet to fulfill, in part, the Library's mission of promoting full and equal access to information and ideas, the love of reading, the joy of learning, and engagement with the arts, sciences and humanities.

Hennepin County Library supports the right to privacy and confidentiality of Library customers in accordance with the Minnesota Data Practices Act. The content of the Internet is not managed or governed by any entity; therefore customers may encounter materials they consider offensive.

Parents and guardians are responsible for monitoring Internet access for their children ages 17 and under.

Hennepin County, Hennepin County Library, Hennepin County Library Board and its employees assume no responsibility for damages of any type arising from the use of Internet workstations.

Illegal use of the Internet is prohibited.

It is illegal for library customers to use the Library's Internet access to view, print, distribute, display, send or receive images, or graphics of material that violates laws relating to child pornography.

Library customers may not knowingly exhibit or display any material which is harmful to minors in its content or material that is obscene in any place of public accommodation where minors are or may be present and where minors are able to view the material.

Workstations are equipped with software that filters out pornography.

Minnesota Statutes 13.40 (Minnesota Data Practices Act); 134.50 (Internet access, libraries); 617.241 (Obscene material); 617.246 (Child Pornography); 617.292 (Materials harmful to minors)

---

behavior policies, they really outline what is unacceptable. This gives the staff freedom and authority to deal with disruptive behavior and take appropriate action. Figure 5.7 is a policy from the Thomas Branigan Memorial Library in Las Cruces, New Mexico. This policy clearly states what is not allowed and even includes local ordinances that enforce acceptable behaviors. The policy also gives clear authority to the staff for taking action.

- **Sponsorship policy**. Increasingly, libraries are partnering with local businesses and civic organizations to provide new equipment, collections, and services. Without a good, clear policy, however, a potential sponsor can get a lot more than they are paying for in terms of marketing. The Norfolk Public Library in Virginia has a sponsorship policy that recognizes the right of sponsors to be acknowledged for their gifts, but keeps the library in the forefront and minimizes the commercial nature of any gift (Figure 5.8). In addition, the policy makes it clear that the library and not the donor will make decisions for implementation and will not breech library policy in exchange for gifts and sponsorships.

Figure 5.6. Circulation Policy, Oliver Wolcott Library (Litchfield, CT)

Oliver Wolcott Library
Circulation Policy

Free and Equal Access to Library Material and Services

It is the policy of the Oliver Wolcott Library, as approved by the Board of Trustees, that the Library shall include in its Circulation Policy the American Library Association's Library Bill of Rights (1980), its Freedom to Read Statement (1972), and its related intellectual freedom documents. These documents endorse free and equal access to library material and services for all people, regardless of race, creed, national origin, age, place of residence, or other personal criteria. It is the policy of the Oliver Wolcott Library not to forbid or impede the circulation of items from the Library collection to any of its cardholders in good standing, whether resident or non-resident, based upon that cardholder's race, creed, national origin, age, place of residence, or other personal criteria. It is the policy of the Oliver Wolcott Library that parents or guardians, not Library staff or Trustees, are responsible for monitoring and approving the selection of material made by children. It is the parents or guardians, and only these, who may restrict their children, and only their children, from access to Library material and/or services, including access to the internet. Parents or guardians who wish their children not to have access to certain material or services should so advise and supervise their children.

Registration

An Oliver Wolcott Library card may be used to borrow materials at any public library in the state of Connecticut that participates in the Connecticard Library Service Program. Any person eighteen years of age or older, or the parent/guardian of any person under eighteen years of age, with an Oliver Wolcott Library card is responsible for all charged materials, associated fees, and notification of card loss or change of address.

All cards are free of charge. A $1.00 fee will be assessed for any lost cards.

Residents and Taxpayers: Any person who is a resident or taxpayer of the Town of Litchfield (including Bantam, Northfield and Milton) are eligible to have a library card. The person must present identification (such as a valid drivers license or a post-marked envelope) showing a current Litchfield address or taxpayer status. Library cards are valid for four years.

Teacher Cards: Teachers who teach at a public or private grade school located in Litchfield are eligible for a special library card. These cards are granted for one year, may be renewed annually, and can only be used at the Oliver Wolcott Library. Applicants must provide proof of employment.

Student residents: Students who live at a private school located in Litchfield are eligible for a special student library card. These cards are granted for one year, may be renewed annually, and can only be used at the Oliver Wolcott Library. Applicants must provide proof of residency at the school and a statement signed by the school administrator authorizing the student to obtain a special card and guaranteeing responsibility for material lost or damaged while checked out by the student.

Out-of-state residents: Any out-of-state resident for whom Litchfield is a temporary place of residency may be issued a temporary library card upon request for up to one year and with an annual $25 non-refundable deposit. The applicant must provide both a permanent out-of-state address and phone number as well as a temporary local address and phone number. An out-of-state temporary library card is only valid at the Oliver Wolcott Library.

(Continued)

Figure 5.6. Circulation Policy, Oliver Wolcott Library (Litchfield, CT) (Continued)

Reserves, Interlibrary Loans, Requests for Purchase

Reserves: Materials (except reference materials and serials) that are "on order" or in circulation may be reserved.

Loans placed through our shared network of about 50 Connecticut libraries (Bibliomation Global): Items may be requested from libraries that belong to our shared network in the Bibliomation consortium free of charge. These requests need to be placed by the patron online from a computer (either at home or on one of the library's public-access computers). Intra-library loans will be automatically filled by any Bibliomation library with an available copy. It will be delivered to the Oliver Wolcott Library for the requesting patron and can be returned to any public library. Staff involvement is minimal. As a result, we are able to offer this service for unlimited requests free of charge to all patrons.

Loans placed through the Out-of-Network ReQuest iconn catalog: This catalog is out of our shared network, has state-required staff management, and will be subject to a charge. All inter-library loan materials must be returned to the library where the request was initiated. Patrons requesting inter-library loans are responsible for following up on requests and returning the material promptly. Renewals are at the discretion of the original library. If granted, renewals are for two weeks. Inter-library loans through the statewide system require a large amount of staff time for each request. The state requires certain procedures be followed and requests (even when placed online by the patron) must be submitted and documented by the library staff. As a result, the library allows each patron one inter-library loan request per month for free. Every additional request will incur a nonrefundable service charge of $1.00 per item. Payment must be made in advance. We will process requests as soon as payment has been received. Special loans requiring out-of-state, university, and/or special format (non-book) requests are sometimes subject to an additional charge by the lending library. In these instances, the patron will be notified prior to the fulfillment of the request of the charge and is required to pay the charge if they want the request to be continued. Community and library-sponsored book clubs may place one title request for 10 copies or less of the same title each month at no charge. The contact person for any community book club must fill out a simple form in order to initiate this service. The form is available at the front desk.

Request for Purchase: Anyone may request an item for purchase for the collection. All requests will be reviewed according to the Oliver Wolcott Library Selection Policy. Requested items that are purchased will be placed on reserve for the requesting patron.

Connecticard Library Service Program

The Oliver Wolcott Library complies with the Connecticard guidelines as adopted by the Connecticut State Library. Any materials may be returned to any participating Connecticard library. The borrower is responsible for the materials until they are returned to the owning library.

Overdue Materials

The Oliver Wolcott Library maintains a "No Fines" policy for overdue items as long as they are returned to the Library in good condition. In lieu of fines, voluntary contributions to the Conscience Box will be encouraged and gratefully accepted. As a courtesy, the Library attempts to reach patrons about overdue materials. Borrowers are responsible for returning materials on time and in good condition.

(Continued)

Figure 5.6. Circulation Policy, Oliver Wolcott Library (Litchfield, CT) *(Continued)*

Suspension of Library Borrowing Privileges

A patron's borrowing privileges will be suspended if an item is more than 25 days overdue. Delinquent accounts may be forwarded to another agency for collection. Borrowing privileges will be reinstated when the overdue item or items are either returned in good condition or paid for. However, in cases of continued misuse of borrowing privileges, the Library Director may suspend that borrower's privileges for an indefinite period. Every effort will be made to handle suspension of borrowing privileges with the utmost discretion and courtesy. Such suspension is not meant as a punitive measure. Rather, suspension is viewed as a necessary measure in order to sustain availability of library materials for all patrons.

Lost or Damaged Materials

The fee for replacing an item which is lost or damaged beyond repair is the current replacement cost of the item. Out-of-print materials from the collection incur a fee of $25 or the current replacement cost, whichever amount is higher. Receipts will be issued upon receipt of fee payment. After payment of a fee, a damaged item may be kept by the patron. Refunds for found items are not possible. The Library is not responsible for any damage to patrons' electronic equipment, including but not limited to video recorders, DVD players, audiocassette players, CD players, etc., incurred while playing Library-provided material.

Loans

The circulating collection is available for loan. An item in circulation is considered on loan until it is returned intact. Adult reference materials are available for overnight loan at the discretion of the Library Director or Reference Librarian. Library material may be renewed one time unless a hold has been placed on the item by another patron. Recognizing that the Library seeks to provide equitable access to its materials for all patrons, patrons may borrow a reasonable number of items as determined by the Library staff.

Loan Periods

New adult fiction and non-fiction books 14 days

Adult books including large print 28 days

Children's books 28 days

Audio books (CD and cassette) 14 days

Feature films on video or DVD 7 days

Non-fiction video or DVD 14 days

Music CDs 14 days

Magazines 7 days

Adopted March 18, 2003
Revised 1/10/06
Revised 7/18/06
Revised 1/16/07

Figure 5.7. Patron Behavior Policy, Thomas Branigan Memorial Library (Las Cruces, NM)

Thomas Branigan Memorial Library
Patron Behavior Policy

Lead Unit: Library/Administration
Effective Date: 6 Nov 2005
Review Date: 6 Oct 2005
Number: 1.4
Name: Fermin Rubio
Title: City Attorney

A. PURPOSE

Thomas Branigan Memorial Library is a place where people come to select materials, do research, study, read, and attend programs and meetings. These rules for behavior and conduct are to:

- Protect the rights of individuals who are in the library to use library materials and/or services;
- Protect the rights of staff members to conduct library business without interference;
- Ensure the safety of library users and staff; and
- Preserve library materials and facilities.

B. POLICY STATEMENT

Your entrance to this public library indicates that you are willing and able to act courteously toward all other persons here, act respectfully with regard to public property, and follow all rules of the facility. When socially unacceptable or illegal behavior occurs in the Library it will be dealt with immediately. Violations of the policy are subject to the provision of City Manager Policy 3.9 "Ban From Public Facilities Policy."

To ensure your visit here is safe and enjoyable, the following are prohibited:

- Physically, sexually, or verbally abusing or harassing others. This includes paying unwanted attention to others such as initiating unwanted conversation with another library user or employee, stalking patrons or staff, staring at other patrons or staff for long periods of time, or touching other patrons or staff;
- Defacing, destroying, or tampering with property or equipment;
- Behaving in a disorderly, loud, or disruptive manner;
- Soliciting funds, panhandling, gambling, selling, advertising, petitioning for contributions or support, distributing flyers in the parking lot without a permit, campaigning or proselytizing in the library or on library grounds;

The distribution of leaflets on library property is limited to the community information racks. Local not-for-profit organizations may give literature to the Circulation Department for display. Groups using a meeting room may distribute leaflets in the meeting room during their meetings.

- Interfering with others' use of the library through poor personal hygiene;
- Leaving children under the age of eight or vulnerable adults unsupervised or unattended or otherwise violating the provisions of the Library Policy on Unattended Children;

(Continued)

**Figure 5.7. Patron Behavior Policy, Thomas Branigan Memorial Library
(Las Cruces, NM)** *(Continued)*

For purposes of this policy "unattended" means that the person responsible for the child or vulnerable adult is not within their sight.

- Bringing animals, other than service and therapy animals, into the library;
- Using any form of tobacco in the library;
- Blocking aisles or doors or leaving personal items unattended at any time;
- Using public restrooms to bathe, shave, change/wash clothes or utensils;
- Failing to wear shirts or shoes;
- Using cell phones in the Library (except for authorized City personnel conducting City business);
- Running in the library;
- Possessing, selling, or using alcoholic beverages or illegal substances on library property;
- Sleeping in the library building;
- Carrying a weapon unless authorized by law;
- Using radios, tape players, or other personal listening equipment at a level that can be heard by others;
- Skateboarding, roller-skating, or rollerblading in the library;
- Failing to adhere to library policies;
- Interfering with another person's use of the library or with the library personnel's performance of their duties;
- Using the emergency exits other than during an emergency;
- Entering unauthorized workspaces or office areas;
- Eating in the Library except in staff areas and for groups meeting in the Meeting Room. Covered beverages are permitted.

Library staff have the right to:

- Require that an individual return to the check out desk if the security gates sound an alarm;
- Restrict the length of time an individual may use library equipment;
- Make decisions that are in the best interests of the library; and
- Require individuals violating library policies to leave.

The library reserves the right to inspect all bags, purses, briefcases, packs, personal listening equipment, etc. for library materials.

Patron use of library telephones

Library telephones are for Official City Business. The main library has a public pay telephone in the foyer. Children who need to contact a parent or other caregiver may use the telephone at the children's desk, with staff permission. Calls are limited to three minutes or less.

C. APPLICABILITY

This policy applies to all persons in Thomas Branigan Memorial Library and on Library premises.

(Continued)

Figure 5.7. Patron Behavior Policy, Thomas Branigan Memorial Library (Las Cruces, NM) *(Continued)*

D. LEGAL REFERENCES

Las Cruces Municipal Code (LCMC)

General Provisions

Sec. 1-10 General penalty for violations; injunctive relief authorized

Advertising

Sec. 3-42 Restricted in public places

Alcoholic Beverages

Sec. 5-1 Drinking or possessing in public

Health and Human Services

Sec. 12-124 Smoking in public places

Human Rights

Sec. 14-26 Purpose (nondiscrimination)

Nuisances

Sec. 18-1 Definitions

Sec. 18-3 Prohibited (creation or maintenance of a nuisance)

Offenses and Miscellaneous Provisions

Sec. 19-4 Concealing identity

Sec. 19-36 Criminal damage to property

Sec. 19-37 Larceny

Sec. 19-38 Fraud

Sec. 19-42 Criminal trespass

Sec. 19-47 Falsely obtaining services or accommodations

Sec. 19-51 Library property

Sec. 19-52 Graffiti vandalism

Sec. 19-81 Assault

Sec. 19-82 Battery

Offenses and Miscellaneous Provisions *(Continued)*

Sec. 19-83 Domestic violence

Sec. 19-84 Same—Barricade of residence or taking of hostage

Sec. 19-85 Public affray

Sec. 19-87 Disorderly conduct

Sec. 19-88 Disturbing lawful assembly

Sec. 19-90 Obstructing movement

Sec. 19-91 Use of telephone to terrify, intimidate, threaten, harass, annoy or offend

Sec. 19-92 Harassment and stalking

Sec. 19-134 Temporary permits

Sec. 19-161 Definitions

Sec. 19-162 Exception for peace officers

Sec. 19-163 Unlawful carrying of a deadly weapon

Sec. 19-165 Unlawful possession of switchblades

Sec. 19-166 Brass or metal knuckles or bludgeons

Sec. 19-201 Indecent exposure

Peddlers and Itinerant Merchants

Sec. 21-62 Prohibited solicitations

Sec. 21-64 Penalties

City Manager Policy 3.9 Ban From Public Facilities Policy

All other applicable City Manager Policies, Library Policies, State or Federal Laws.

E. APPEALS PROCESS

Pursuant to the Ban From Public Facilities Policy, CMP# 3.9 all incidents will be documented on an incident report and dealt with immediately. The next higher level of authority shall review the incident and the action taken. Immediate suspension can be appealed to the Public Services Director. Suspension by the Director can be appealed to the Library Advisory Board. Suspension by the Advisory Board may be appealed to the City Council.

F. RESPONSIBILITY

Library Staff are authorized to bring to an individual's attention any act or omission that violates these rules and detracts from the decorum of the library. Staff are authorized to enforce these rules courteously, but firmly.

Figure 5.8. Sponsorship Policy and Procedures, Norfolk Public Library System (Norfolk, VA)

Norfolk Public Library System
Sponsorship
Policy and Procedures

The Norfolk Public Library welcomes sponsorship from local business, corporations, families and individuals. The aim of sponsorship is to obtain funding or in-kind support to provide services and equipment that may not otherwise be available. The Board of Trustees of the Norfolk Public Library believes that libraries play an essential role in the quality of life of our citizens and in this important function, the library should be supported through public funding. Therefore, sponsorship revenue should only be used to fund optional additional services or new, "start up" services.

Guiding Principles

The following principles will guide the Norfolk Public Library in the solicitation and acceptance of gifts, grants or support to enhance or develop library programs and services:

- All gifts, grants and/or support must further the library's mission, goals, objectives and priorities. They must not drive the library's agenda or priorities.
- All gifts, grants and/or support must safeguard equity of access to library services. Sponsorship agreements must not give unfair advantage to, or cause discrimination against, sectors of the community.
- All gifts, grants and/or support must protect the principle of intellectual freedom. Sponsors may not direct the selection of collections or require endorsement of products or services.
- All gifts, grants and/or support must ensure the confidentiality of user records. The library will not sell or provide access to library records in exchange for gifts or support.
- All gifts, grants and/or support must leave open the opportunity for other actual or potential donors to have similar opportunities to provide support to the library.
- Gifts of books or other library materials will be accepted in accordance with the terms outlined in the NPL Collection Development Policy.

Recognition and Acknowledgement

The library will ensure that each sponsor receives acknowledgement and to the degree that the donor is willing, public recognition. The following guidelines will be used in providing acknowledgement to and recognition for sponsors:

- A letter of acknowledgement for gifts of money and in-kind support will be sent to all sponsors and a copy will be placed on file.
- Any special recognition agreements will be stipulated in the letter.
- Public acknowledgement of sponsorship in the library's promotional materials will normally be restricted to a statement of the sponsor's name and a display of logo. Standards controlling the size, format and location of such acknowledgment will be developed by the public information specialist to ensure both consistency and quality of appearance. Such acknowledgement will not take precedence or have prominence over the library's own logo or promotional material.
- For gifts and/or sponsorships valued at over $500, the library may submit a press release to local newspapers and/or publish an article regarding the sponsorship in their own newsletter if the sponsor is willing.

(Continued)

Figure 5.8. Sponsorship Policy and Procedures, Norfolk Public Library System (Norfolk, VA) *(Continued)*

- Acknowledgement of sponsorship may also take the following forms at the library's discretion:
  - Launch of a special program or media campaign to announce the gift.
  - Sponsor's name on promotional materials.
  - Small standardized plaques may be placed on donated furniture or equipment.
  - Library bookplates.

In all cases, the type and scope of donor recognition required by the donor will be weighed against the benefit to the library.

Approval

- All gifts, grants or in-kind support given with special requirements must be approved by the Director of Libraries. The solicitation of gifts, grants or in-kind support by library staff and valued at over $500 must receive prior approval of the Director of Libraries. All gifts valued at $5,000 or more must be accepted by ordinance through the Norfolk City Council per city regulations.

Authority for Implementation

- The library reserves the right to make decisions regarding the implementation of each grant, gift, or offer of in-kind support. Purchasing decisions, including type of equipment, materials, furnishings, and other components of a gift will reside with library management. All details as to design of programs and allocation of resources will also reside with library management.

6

Doing It Right: The Best Practices of Effective Library Boards

Board Member Orientation

Great library trustees are not born, they are made. Very few library trustees attend their first board meeting with a lot of experience and knowledge about the library they are serving. Many won't be aware of the wide variety of services the library offers or even the kinds of resources that are needed to deliver these services. They are unlikely to be fully aware of their role and what will be expected of them.

Each new trustee should get a tour of the library and an opportunity to meet some of the staff. Additionally, each new board member should be assigned a mentor from among existing board members. A good mentor will take time to visit with a new trustee to explain the board culture, the role of the board (especially versus the role of the director), and the various ways in which the new trustee can be productive. The mentor should also talk informally about what is on the horizon for the library. Is the board thinking about a new building project? Will there be a budget battle in the fall? Is a new planning process underway? What are the values that are reflected in the library's mission and vision statements? All of this will go a long way to ensure that the new trustee is able to be a contributing and valuable member beginning with his or her very first meeting.

Orientation Packet

When a new trustee is appointed or elected, he or she should receive a package of information that will begin the education process. New trustees should be highly encouraged to go through all of the information in the packet before meeting a board mentor. A strong cover letter extolling the important role trustees play in governing the library and conveying the board's expectation that all materials sent out in advance of meetings are read by all board members will begin to acquaint the new member with your expectations. Included in the orientation should be the following:

- A welcome letter from the board president congratulating the new trustee and underlining the importance of this position. The cover letter should include the expectation that the materials included in the packet be read, the date of the next board meeting, the name and contact information of the board mentor (if applicable), a brief overview of how often the board meets including where and when, and contact information for the library director.

- A copy of the conflict of interest policy and the ethics statement for signature.

- Bylaws, mission, vision, and planning documents. These will help the new trustee understand how the board works, the library's highest values (mission and vision), and what goals the library has embraced to move forward.

- Local and state laws that govern the library. All trustees should know about laws that will impact both the board's and the library's operations. In all cases, the local and state laws will supersede library policy and may dictate board responsibilities as well as how trustees are selected for service.

- Minutes from board meetings of the past year. These minutes will give a good sense of how your meetings are run and the types of issues that are discussed. Also, included in the minutes will be discussions of concerns, and subsequent minutes should reflect how these were resolved. The minutes will allow a sort of fly-on-the-wall look into the board's recent past operations.

- A list of all current trustees, their office (if any), and their contact information.

- The policy manual. Nothing will be more informative to a new trustee than seeing exactly how a library is governed. Because good policies include a statement about the purpose of each policy, this will help underline that the board attempts to ensure that library services are distributed in a fair and equal manner. The policies themselves will indicate who is responsible for implementation, further helping the new trustee to understand the role of the trustee versus that of the staff.

- Information about the library. This should include a brief history, a staff organizational chart, information on the library's size—if a system, how many branches and where they are located, a copy of the library's budget, the annual report for the last two years, and use statistics for the three prior years.

- Promotional material from the library including copies of recent newsletters, program flyers, bookmarks, Web site information, and so forth.

- A copy of this book!

All of this is a lot to go through, it's true, and it can be a bit overwhelming. But without a good grounding through orientation, you are very likely to be continually educating a new trustee, and that can cause misunderstandings and unhappiness. Much like a new job in the business world, the first impression is the most important one of all and can influence a person's behavior and commitment for years to come.

Board Meetings

While it might not seem glamorous, the truth is that the majority of time a board member spends in service to the library will be at the monthly board meeting. It is important, therefore, that these meetings are structured in a way that ensures they are productive and allow for the intellectual input of all board members in determining how well the library is meeting its obligations to the citizens it serves.

Operating Procedure

The board president who presides over the meeting (or the vice president in the absence of the president) should be well acquainted with meeting rules. How many trustees must be present to constitute a quorum? How will decisions be made—by a majority or by consensus? When will a trustee be considered out of order? How can everyone be brought into critical discussions? Your bylaws will answer some of these questions (see Chapter 1). In addition, there are many books available that can help guide you, including books on proper parliamentary procedure, perhaps the most famous of which are *Robert's Rules of Order* and *The Standard Code of Parliamentary Procedure* by Alice Sturgis.

Attendance

Does it really matter? Yes! Because board meetings are where trustees are kept up to date on issues such as budget, services, staff, and policy—and because they are ultimately accountable for the responsible stewardship of these issues—it is imperative that all board members are required to attend. The board bylaws should stipulate the number of unexcused absences and excused absences that will be permitted.

An unexcused absence occurs when the trustee simply does not show up and has not notified anyone in advance. A good policy might excuse one of these absences since life does happen and people do sometimes forget. However, if the trustee isn't serious enough about his or her service to the library to schedule time for board meetings or make a call to inform either the board president or the library director that he or she can't make the meeting, it may be that the seat would be better filled by someone who is.

An excused absence occurs when the board member has called ahead and asked to be excused because of illness, travel, or other unforeseen conflict. Though there are many good reasons for missing a meeting, consistent absences should be considered unacceptable because it means that a seat that would otherwise be filled by a dependable person goes empty too often. Again, a good policy stipulating that one or two excused absences is acceptable in a year along with stating the procedure for removing a board member who is unable to comply is important.

It is, of course, not enough for a trustee to simply show up. He or she should be expected to contribute to discussions and should be required to have read the board packet in advance (see the section Board Packet on p. 95). Good board members show up prepared to contribute.

Agenda

A good agenda is the best tool you have for ensuring that a meeting goes smoothly, that all issues of importance are adequately addressed, and that everyone has an opportunity to contribute thoughts and ideas (for an example agenda, see Figure 6.1).

The board president and the library director should work together on the agenda for each meeting well in advance. The library director will know best what items are hot at the moment and need to be addressed, and the board president may have issues he or she would like to discuss in the meeting. In addition to these new business items, there will be some standard agenda items such as a

---

Figure 6.1. Sample Library Board of Trustees Meeting Agenda

Anytown Public Library Board of Trustees Meeting Agenda

Date: Mon., Sept. 21, 2009
Time: 5:30–7 p.m.
Location: Central Library, Donnell Meeting Room
Meeting begins promptly at 5:30 p.m.

Welcome and introductions (5 minutes)

Approval of the minutes (5 minutes) **Action Item**

Director's report: Bill Jones (15 minutes)

- New services
- Use statistics

Budget review: Karen Smith, Treasurer (10 minutes)

Policy update: Collections (20 minutes) **Action Item**

Advocacy efforts: preparing for next year's budget (15 minutes)

Friends report (5 minutes)

Foundation report (5 minutes)

Public comment (10 minutes)

Adjournment at 7 p.m.

year-to-date budget report, library use statistics, opportunity for public comment, and a state of the library update from the director. Other issues that might be on a standard agenda are reports by a Friends of the Library and/or foundation liaison.

To maximize the time available to discuss the most important items on the agenda, those that are fairly standard and don't require an action (such as a vote) or discussion can be grouped together as a consent agenda. If the budget is tracking well, the use of the library is steady or normal, and the Friends liaison has submitted a written report in lieu of attending, for example, these items can be grouped together for approval in one motion. Of course, any item in the consent agenda can be pulled out for discussion or action if a particular trustee requests it. If the board is unanimous in accepting the consent agenda, however, time will be freed up for the issues that do require action and/or discussion.

Another way to help move the agenda along is to mark those items that need action. This way there will be a clear understanding at a glance that the discussion at hand will be leading to a vote. Approval of the minutes, approval of a new policy proposal, or a change in the board's operating procedures are examples of those that will require action.

Finally, manage the clock. Decide when the meeting will begin and end, and include that information in the agenda. Each item on the agenda should be accorded a certain amount of time. These times should be flexible, of course, but if you've allotted five minutes for welcomes and introductions and you notice that almost ten minutes have gone by, you will know that it is time to firmly and gracefully bring this item to a close. The suggested time limits for each item will also help keep all trustees focused and on track.

Board Packet

The board packet is developed by library staff and sent out to each member of the board so that it is received at least one week prior to the meeting. The board packet should contain helpful background information that supports the items of the agenda. Standard information usually includes the following:

- **Agenda**. This should be the top page of the board packet. It includes the date, time, and location for the upcoming board meeting and quickly gives an overview of what will be discussed and decided.

- **Minutes**. The board's secretary (and this may be a library staff member who serves as secretary ex officio but has no vote) should ensure that minutes are sent to the director no later than one week following the meeting. The minutes may be distributed to the full board simultaneously after the meeting, but a written copy should still be included in the packet.

- **State of the library report**. The director should include a short (one or two page) summary of significant issues and trends that have occurred since the last board meeting. This report should address key issues and not get bogged down with a lot of details. The shorter and more concise this report, the more likely it will be read and will be valuable in focusing the board members on what really matters.

- **Budget report.** A useful report will show the library's expenditures to date versus the same time last year. It is also useful to see a report that compares expenditures to date versus the annual budget.

- **Library use statistics.** Use statistics don't necessarily measure a library's effectiveness; they can, however, highlight trends. Reports that show various measures of use against prior months and prior years give context to the data and help to show more clearly the changes occurring in the ways in which patrons are using the library.

In addition to these standard reports, the board packet might also include these items:

- **Policy update.** It is good practice for a board to review all the library's policies at least biennially. This doesn't mean that policies should change every year or every two years, but they should be reviewed on a regular basis to make sure they are still guiding library practice in a way that matches the library's mission and goals.

    If a particular policy is up for review, a copy of the policy should be included in the board packet along with a brief report by the director that recommends modification or states that the policy is relevant as it stands, with explanation of either recommendation. This will give the board members the information they need to reauthorize the policy or to recommend well-thought-out changes.

- **Friends report.** It's important for the trustees to include a report from the Friends group (oral, written, or both) at each meeting. Friends are a significant factor in fund-raising efforts, library promotion, and advocacy, so it makes sense that the trustees are kept aware of their activities. In addition, including a Friends liaison and/or report strengthens the bond between the two groups, making it much easier to coordinate advocacy and promotion efforts.

- **Foundation report.** Typically, library foundations work to foster large gifts and donations from wealthy individuals and corporations for the library endowment. Often this is done through planned giving, ticketed events, grant writing, and one-to-one requests. It is common for a board member to be on the foundation board. If this is the case, he or she might give an update, or the foundation president might include a written report for the board packet.

- **Articles of interest.** A high-functioning board is one that understands the broader context within which the library operates. The library director should keep the board informed of issues that impact libraries, whether they are at the national, state, or local level. Pertinent articles and papers on these issues should be included with an explanation of their import during the director's report.

Effective meetings can move the organization forward. By spending this precious time in discussing policy issues, environmental concerns (what factors are affecting the library such as funding, population shifts, and political environment), and library goals, the trustees can be a real boon to the director and to the community.

Board Self-Evaluation

Trustees make important fiscal and administrative decisions critical to the functioning of their library. Board members commit their time and skills for effective governing. It is important that they understand their roles and responsibilities and possess the information necessary to make wise decisions as a board. Figure 6.2 includes general areas for assessment and sample questionnaires within each area to help highlight areas of strength and weakness.

Figure 6.2. Library Board Self-Evaluation

General Knowledge

To be truly effective, board members must understand their role versus that of the director. Each trustee should also understand the role of the library itself—the library's mission and how the library's policies, services, and programs work to ensure that the mission is met. Trustees should be well versed on the various issues that impact their library and its services, including issues on the state and national levels such as trends in intellectual freedom, privacy rights, and funding for libraries.

1. Board members understand their roles and responsibilities.
   YES____ NO____

2. Board members understand the role and responsibilities of the library director.
   YES____ NO____

3. Board members can identify the mission statement, objectives and vision of the library.
   YES____ NO____

4. Board members are familiar with all local, state, and federal laws having effect on libraries.
   YES____ NO____

5. Board members are familiar with library issues at the local, state, and federal levels.
   YES____ NO____

6. Board members understand the structure and bylaws of the board.
   YES____ NO____

(Continued)

Figure 6.2. Library Board Self-Evaluation *(Continued)*

General Knowledge *(Continued)*

7. Board members are familiar with current library policies.

   YES____ NO____

8. Board members know which agency (agencies) the board reports to.

   YES____ NO____

Board Operation

Effective board operations do impact the quality of trustee deliberation and decision making (see Board Meetings). The questions below will help trustees assess their ability to hold effective meetings that foster interaction and help to move the library forward.

1. The library director provides the board with accurate and up-to-date information in order to make sound and effective decisions at least one week in advance of meetings.

   YES____ NO____

2. Board members are given an opportunity to express views without prejudice.

   YES____ NO____

3. The board chair sets a clear agenda and circulates it to trustees prior to each meeting.

   YES____ NO____

4. The board chair identifies goals for the meetings and summarizes progress on business at the end.

   YES____ NO____

5. The rules of *Robert's Rules of Order* or similar official parliamentary guide are followed.

   YES____ NO____

6. Board members regularly attend meetings and assigned committee meetings.

   YES____ NO____

Fund-Raising

Because trustees are ultimately accountable for the quality of service their library provides, they must necessarily have a broad view on fund-raising. This begins with understanding the economic environment within which the library operates. It also means that they are aware of the various opportunities that exist for bringing in additional resources. The trustees, working with the library director, can set goals for fund-raising and, importantly, assist in the attainment of those goals.

1. The board assists in setting fund-raising goals and is actively involved in fund-raising.

   YES____ NO____

2. The board initiates fund-raising campaigns with the cooperation of the library director and follows through with implementation.

   YES____ NO____

(Continued)

Figure 6.2. Library Board Self-Evaluation *(Continued)*

Fund-Raising *(Continued)*

3. The board is aware of the funding needs of the library.

   YES____ NO____

4. Board members make connections with the corporate community and communicate these connections to the board.

   YES____ NO____

5. Board members liaise with the Friends of the Library.

   YES____ NO____

6. If a Friends group does not exist, the board provides assistance in establishing such a group and in maintaining a supportive relationship.

   YES____ NO____

Advocacy

No one has a stronger and more well-informed voice than the library's trustees. They have the benefit of understanding exactly what the library provides to the community and what it takes to provide services. In addition, unlike staff, the trustees have nothing to gain personally from strong financial support.

1. Board members are cognizant of the political process and the manner in which the board can impact decision making.

   YES____ NO____

2. Board members accept and respect that the chair is the lead spokesperson for the board.

   YES____ NO____

3. The library director works with the board to develop a strong message and talking points.

   YES____ NO____

4. The board liaises with the press on a regular basis.

   YES____ NO____

5. The board pursues advocacy initiatives year round—before, during, and after elections.

   YES____ NO____

6. The board develops a long-range plan for advocacy on a year-round basis.

   YES____ NO____

7. All board members take an active part in advocating for the library.

   YES____ NO____

8. Board members are given the necessary information to contact elected officials during the year and keep such officials or other informal contacts informed on library issues through visitations, e-mails, and phone calls.

   YES____ NO____

(Continued)

Figure 6.2. Library Board Self-Evaluation (Continued)

Advocacy (Continued)

9. Board members make visits to community groups for the purpose of articulating the library's role and contribution to the community.

   YES____ NO____

10. The board actively lobbies decision makers and/or the community at large for support of the budget each year.

    YES____ NO____

Strategic Planning

Even if the library wanted to maintain the status quo, the environment within which the library operates is constantly changing. That means that in order for the library to effectively deliver services to its community, the board must ensure that the library's mission and goals are always relevant. Strategic planning, therefore, is an important job for trustees.

1. The board creates goals and action plans based on the strategic plan.

   YES____ NO____

2. The board reviews progress of the plan on a regular basis.

   YES____ NO____

3. An orientation package containing the current strategic plan is provided for new board members.

   YES____ NO____

4. Strategic planning becomes a regular process for the board.

   YES____ NO____

Policymaking

All boards must be familiar with library policy and, importantly, with the reasoning behind each policy. If policies are challenged, board members must be able to explain them and stand behind them.

1. The board reviews policies on an annual basis.

   YES____ NO____

2. The board is familiar with policies.

   YES____ NO____

3. The board can articulate the underlying principle(s) that the policy is addressing and is able to defend the policies to the public.

   YES____ NO____

4. Board members can distinguish between policymaking and operational decision making.

   YES____ NO____

(Continued)

Figure 6.2. Library Board Self-Evaluation (Continued)

Finance

In most libraries, the financial responsibility of the board is oversight. Day-to-day decision making regarding the dispensation of the library's resources rightfully belongs with the library director. This does not mean, however, that the board can abdicate their responsibility to ensure that the budget is being spent appropriately and that the budget is working in support of the library's mission and goals.

1. The board is provided with full and accurate information regarding the library's finances and budget throughout the year.

   YES___ NO___

2. The board is given sufficient lead-in time to discuss budget issues and make wise decisions.

   YES___ NO___

3. The board understands the impact of decisions on the enhancement of services.

   YES___ NO___

4. The board is prepared and motivated to defend and promote the budget to the decision makers.

   YES___ NO___

5. The information provided reflects back to specific services.

   YES___ NO___

Professional Development

The best boards around are those that continue to learn and grow in their roles. There are many ways to do this. The very first step in providing each trustee with the knowledge he or she needs to be effective begins with board orientation. Other steps can be as easy as joining regional and state library associations that have special sections for trustees. Attending national or state conferences where programs for trustees are presented is another opportunity for continuing education.

1. Board members are given opportunities at the local, state. and national level to improve performance.

   YES___ NO___

2. Board members are encouraged by the chair to take on such opportunities.

   YES___ NO___

3. Board members are given an opportunity to report back and share with other board members information acquired.

   YES___ NO___

4. New members are given a board orientation on their roles.

   YES___ NO___

(Continued)

Figure 6.2. Library Board Self-Evaluation *(Continued)*

Professional Development

5. Board members are members of local, state, and/or national associations (Association of Library Trustees, Advocates, Friends and Foundations, Public Library Association, etc.).

   YES___ NO___

Once the responses have been compiled, you should be able to see what you are doing well and what areas need to be addressed so that you can be a highly effective and productive team.

_____

This Board evaluation document was produced for ALTAFF under the leadership of Nicholas Spillios (Alberta, Canada Library Trustees), Donna McDonald (Library Director, Arkansas River Valley Regional Library System), and Alan Smith (Trustee, Contra Costa, California, County Library).

7

Today's and Tomorrow's Concerns: Key Issues Facing Libraries

As trustees, it is very important to be aware of the policy issues and trends that have an impact on your library. You may never have to face a challenge of your library collection or be asked by your city manager to look into outsourcing the management of your library, but it's important to know about these issues and trends so that you can have policies in place to back you up when you are faced with defending your collections and services.

In addition to the trend to reduce or eliminate library funding at locales across the country (see Chapter 2), other important issues face public libraries today. Some are fairly new, such as the privatization of libraries, but others are perennial. All deserve a place on your agenda for policy discussions because they greatly impact your ability to serve all the people in your community in an environment that is private and nonjudgmental and fosters the free flow of information so critical to a democracy.

Intellectual Freedom

Our forefathers believed so strongly that rights of individuals should not be at the mercy of a tyrannical government that they developed the Bill of Rights just after adopting the U.S. Constitution. The preamble of the Bill of Rights says this:

> The Conventions of a number of the States, having at the time of their adopting the Constitution, expressed a desire, *in order to prevent misconstruction or abuse of its powers*, that further declaratory and restrictive clauses should be added: And as extending the ground of public confidence in the Government, will best ensure the beneficent ends of its institution. [emphasis added]

It is likely no mistake that the very first of these rights is the freedom of religion, speech, the press, and assembly. In other words, it is critical to our democracy that people have the freedom to think, believe, say, and write what they want. It is a precious freedom, and one that has been closely guarded for over two centuries.

In libraries, this freedom plays out on a daily basis. Collection policies in libraries almost always state a commitment to a wide diversity of ideas and thoughts. For too many, this is a dangerous concept. There are those who believe that some thoughts, rather than actions based on thought, have no place in a library where anyone could read, view, or hear them. These people would gladly have titles removed from the library's shelves and often take action to do just that.

It is not unlikely that if your library's collection truly is diverse and reflective of the full spectrum of belief in your community, you will someday be faced with a challenge. These challenges can come from an individual or a group and can escalate beyond the grievance procedure you have in place (see page 76 for a sample Reconsideration of Library Materials form, and ALA materials in Appendix B).

As guardians of the public's trust, it is up to your board to face such challenges and, importantly, uphold the rights of all people to have access to the wide range of materials and subjects represented in your collection—whether these ideas are popular or not.

This may not be an easy task. Very often, strong emotion surrounds a challenge both in those who would like to see materials removed or restricted and in those who believe that all ideas have a right to be represented in the public library. You will have to work hard to be as dispassionate as you can in the face of challenges, and rely on your policies to back up your commitment to intellectual freedom for all.

Surprisingly, most people, whether conservative or liberal, will defend the principles of intellectual freedom and agree that, even when an idea or position is unpopular, the access to those ideas is more important than keeping certain classes of people "safe" from them. With this in mind, it is often best to let the public know about any serious challenge being made to your library that has escalated past the reconsideration of library materials process. Because the media depends on First Amendment rights, they are likely (but not guaranteed) to be on your side along with others in the community who do not want their right to learn, think about, read, or view abridged in a future challenge.

The Office of Intellectual Freedom of the American Library Association has a wide variety of materials that can help you face a challenge. In addition, they sponsor Banned Books Week each September to highlight the important role that libraries play in safeguarding this important freedom. Their annual list of most challenged titles will astound most library supporters and will show that many of the books that have truly had an impact on our culture are those that show up year after year. These titles include *The Holy Bible*, *The Adventures of Huckleberry Finn* (Mark Twain), *The Color Purple* (Alice Walker), and *The Jungle* (Upton Sinclair), just to name a very few.[1]

User Privacy

The issue of patron privacy is, of course, critical to intellectual freedom. Tracing an individual's use of the library is a little like following along with his or her thinking. The important thing, though, is that trying to understand the workings of another's mind is wide open to misinterpretation and to persecution. No one would feel safe to pursue all the information he or she wanted or needed if there were a sense that others could "look over their shoulders." Believing or knowing that others could access reading or viewing history would no doubt have a chilling effect on someone seeking information, for example, on sexually transmitted diseases, abortion, or any number of legitimate but sensitive topics.

How likely would the teenager be to access materials on sexually transmitted diseases or homosexuality if anyone could see his or her records? How likely would a spouse be to find out about reconciliation after infidelity in a marriage if the pursuit of this information was common knowledge or easily accessed? Not only are issues of a personal nature safeguarded by patron privacy policies, but those investigating unpopular political beliefs or philosophies are protected as well. The protection of privacy ensures that all patrons have unfettered access to the information they want or need.

Most (if not all) states have laws that govern the confidentiality of patron records to uphold the importance of patron privacy. In practice, most libraries delete patron records as soon as materials are returned or a computer search is completed. However, the FBI and other law enforcement agencies have been known to enter libraries without proper subpoenas and demand that public computers be relinquished to them.

Strong policies regarding patron privacy are critical. The Office of Intellectual Freedom at ALA offers a lot of help to libraries that are creating or updating privacy policies.[2] Even in a changing (digital) environment, libraries are still committed to the bedrock principal that patrons do and should always have an expectation of privacy.

Pay Equity for Library Workers

You might think that in a profession dominated by women, female librarians would be earning as much as their male counterparts and be proportionately represented in administrative roles. You might think that, but you'd be wrong.[3] Within our own ranks, we still foster salary inequities. No one is in a better position to ensure that is not the case in your library than the board. Hiring practices and salary offerings should be closely monitored by the board to ensure that your library has not slipped into a pattern of paying more for men than women and is not unfairly discriminating against workers on the basis of race or ethnicity.

In comparison to other professions requiring the same level of education and experience, librarians and library workers continue to lag behind in earnings. In fact, it is undoubtedly because librarianship is still a "woman's profession" that this is the case, since women's wages in America continue to lag behind those of men. In addition, there has been a disturbing trend in cities and towns across the country to "deprofessionalize" librarians' work[4]—handing more and more of it to paraprofessionals who lack the degree and often the expertise to deliver the same level of services, but cost less to employ.

As guardians of the quality of library service, and as committed as you surely are to fair treatment for all the library's employees, it is incumbent upon you to make sure that there is pay equity within the library and outside of it. If yours is a city or county department, it is likely that the library's staff is placed on a scale that purports to place all similarly skilled, educated, experienced workers on the same level.

The fact is, however, that not all the placement criteria are solely objective, and such factors as safety, strength needed, stress level of work performed, and hours worked come into play. Unfortunately, there is still a strong perception in the human resources world that all library workers do is quietly interact with well-heeled patrons and have the opportunity to read in their spare time.

No one knows better than you how untrue this is. Libraries are not inherently safe places (being open to all people at all hours is not a wholly safe situation); they are very stressful for workers who are dealing with increased and increasingly diverse use; they are open at night; and library workers work anything but Monday–Friday, 9 a.m.–5 p.m. shifts. These components of library staff work must be reflected in their rankings within the city or county, or undoubtedly they will be paid less regardless of degree and experience required.

When you advocate for your library, be sure that you advocate for the library's staff. Few trustees would dispute that the staff is the library's most valuable asset. You should work hard to be sure that this asset is treated fairly and paid well.

The Privatization of Public Libraries

That's right—some public libraries across the country are being managed by for-profit companies. These companies, of course, will claim that they can run libraries better and cheaper than is currently the case. They make these claims to city and county governments who are all too happy to wash their hands of the library and save some money to boot. In an effort to save money (while caring little for quality library services or the idea that libraries belong in the public domain), many localities are outsourcing their library services in part or in their entirety.

The fact is, if your library isn't being well managed, you need to do what is necessary to ensure that your library director is either coached to become an excellent manager or leader or is fired so that you can hire someone who is (see Chapter 3).

While the standard is for the private company to hire a professional library manager, that manager reports directly to the company itself. Sure, a library board (now more advisory than anything else) will be left in place but, as they say, follow the money. The director will be directly responsible to the company paying his or her salary, and this is a situation ripe for self-interest.

The beauty of the public library is that it is answerable to the public at large. It will safeguard collections, services, and programs that may not be popular with everyone but that serve the library's critical mission. A library director charged with increasing circulation statistics, for example, by the for-profit company that wants to show how well they are doing would be very tempted to increase high-circulating materials like audiovisual and popular fiction to achieve that even if it's at the expense of materials that serve a smaller diverse population or are used primarily in-house.

In addition, to reduce staff time and costs, a director reporting to a company that is in the business to make money will likely reduce or eliminate outreach services that serve a critical (because isolated) population, but do not reflect well in terms of numbers. However, a library director employed by the city or the library board will have the library and the community at heart in daily decision making.

It doesn't take a lot of critical thinking to understand that a for-profit company must, first and foremost, make a profit. You have to think carefully about what will be eliminated in order to ensure that and to whom your library director will be ultimately accountable—the public the library serves, or the company that writes his or her check.

Notes

1. A complete list can be found at American Library Association, "Banned and Challenged Books," www.ala.org/ala/issuesadvocacy/banned/index.cfm.
2. See American Library Association, "Privacy and Confidentiality," www.ala.org/ala/aboutala/offices/oif/ifissues/privacyconfidentiality.cfm, for sample privacy policies, a guideline to developing privacy policies, and statements on why this is so important.
3. U.S. Department of Commerce, Bureau of the Census, Current Population Survey, Series P-36, 2003; Organization for the Advancement of Library Employees, "Library Workers: Facts and Figures," *Library Worklife* 1, no. 8, www.ala-apa.org/newsletter/vol1no8/salaries.html.
4. Organization for the Advancement of Library Employees, "Library Workers: Facts and Figures," *Library Worklife* 1, no. 8, www.ala-apa.org/newsletter/vol1no8/salaries.html.

Appendix A

A Selected List of Best Sources for Further Reading and Learning

Advocacy

In today's world where the relevance of public libraries is too often in question by those who fund them (though not by those who use them), trustees have a new role to play—that of library advocate. Not only must trustees stay aware of issues at all levels of government that might impact them, they must also fight harder than ever before for a library budget that meets the demands of the community that uses it. There is support for you in this new role. ALA's Washington Office can keep you up to date on national issues and trends, and the ALA Office of Advocacy can also provide you with materials, facts about library impact on communities, and talking points. In addition, there are books and toolkits available that provide veritable blueprints for library advocacy.

- Office of Library Advocacy (ALA): www.ala.org/ala/aboutala/offices/ola/index.cfm
- *Making Our Voices Heard: Citizens Speak Out for Libraries* by Sally Gardner Reed and Beth Nawalinski (Philadelphia: Friends of Libraries U.S.A., 2003)
- *Making the Case for Your Library* by Sally Gardner Reed (New York: Neal-Schuman, 2001)
- Washington Office (ALA): www.ala.org/ala/aboutala/offices/wo/index.cfm

Censorship and Intellectual Freedom

Is your library facing a challenge regarding your materials, meeting room use, displays, or programs? If you need help in a hurry, the best place to go is ALA's Office for Intellectual Freedom. A phone call or e-mail will get you to a knowledgeable staff member who can provide you with advice and resources to help you support your policies, services, and materials. In addition, your state library and your state library association will also be able to help. Your state may even have laws that outline the steps to take when your library and its resources are challenged. Your state library will know if this is the case.

- Office for Intellectual Freedom (ALA): www.ala.org/ala/aboutala/offices/oif/index.cfm
- State library
- State library association

Continuing Education for Trustees

As discussed in Chapter 1, it's important to learn all you can about your important position as trustee along with the issues and trends that impact the library. It's not hard and it doesn't have to cost much—or anything at all. The following resources can help you in the way that works best for you—in print, online, and in person.

- *American Libraries*: www.ala.org/alonline/
- Association for Library Trustees, Advocates, Friends and Foundations: www.ala.org/altaff
- BoardSource: www.boardsource.org
- *Library Journal*: www.libraryjournal.com
- WebJunction: www.webjunction.org
- State library
- State library association

Legal Matters

It might surprise you to learn that there are a variety of laws (mostly at the state level but it's possible that there are city ordinances as well) that will govern certain aspects of your library and its services. Such areas as patron confidentiality, designated service area, nonresident fees, and open meeting requirements are usually prescribed by law and you should know about them. In addition, if your library is a separate 501(c)(3) organization and not a city department, there are federal laws you must obey as well. The people and resources listed here can help to answer general legal questions as regards your library and, in the case of the city or library attorney, questions specific to your particular library.

- *The Nonprofit Legal Landscape* by Ober/Kaler (Washington, DC: BoardSource, 2005)
- State library

- Your city or county attorney
- Your library's attorney

Planning and Policies

Because planning is both important and often overwhelming, it can really help to have some resources or templates to help shepherd you through the process. These resources are especially good and easy to use. In many states, periodic strategic planning is mandated for libraries in order to get state aid. Be sure to find out if this is the case and look to them for planning guides and resources as well.

As the governing board, you will set the framework within which the library director operates on a daily basis. Though you likely won't write policies from scratch (you'll modify, discuss, and approve draft policies presented by the director), you should know the basics so you can determine if the policies do, in fact, address the issues themselves.

- *The Evaluation and Measurement of Library Services* by Joseph R. Mathews (Santa Barbara, CA: Greenwood, 2007)
- *The New Planning for Results: A Streamlined Approach* by Sandra Nelson (Chicago: ALA Editions, 2001)
- *The Public Library Policy Writer* by Jeanette Larson and Herman L. Totten (New York: Neal-Schuman, 2008)
- *The Public Library Data Service (PLDS) Statistical Report*, Public Library Association: www.ala.org/ala/mgrps/divs/pla/plapublications/pldsstatreport/index.cfm
- *Strategic Planning Workbook for Nonprofit Organizations* by Bryan W. Barry (Washington, DC: BoardSource, 2007)
- State library

Working with the Director

As stated in Chapter 4, the library director is your library's most valuable asset. It is incumbent upon the board, therefore, to be absolutely sure that you hire the best person you can find, that you have an evaluation process that is objective and supports continuous improvement, and that you and your director have an honest and open relationship. If you already have all of this in place, congratulations. If not, these resources will surely help.

- *A Library Board's Practical Guide to Finding the Right Library Director* by the Detroit Suburban Librarians' Round Table Succession Planning Committee (Chicago: Public Library Association, 2005)

- *Sample Evaluations of Library Directors* by Sharon Saulmon (Chicago: Association for Library Trustees and Advocates, 1997)

- *Trouble at the Top: The Nonprofit Board's Guide to Managing an Imperfect Chief Executive* by Katha Kissman (Washington, DC: BoardSource, 2009)

Appendix B
Essential Documents Every Trustee Needs

B.1. Libraries: An American Value

Libraries in America are cornerstones of the communities they serve. Free access to the books, ideas, resources, and information in America's libraries is imperative for education, employment, enjoyment, and self-government.

Libraries are a legacy to each generation, offering the heritage of the past and the promise of the future. To ensure that libraries flourish and have the freedom to promote and protect the public good in the twenty-first century, we believe certain principles must be guaranteed.

To that end, we affirm this contract with the people we serve:

- We defend the constitutional rights of all individuals, including children and teenagers, to use the library's resources and services;

- We value our nation's diversity and strive to reflect that diversity by providing a full spectrum of resources and services to the communities we serve;

- We affirm the responsibility and the right of all parents and guardians to guide their own children's use of the library and its resources and services;

- We connect people and ideas by helping each person select from and effectively use the library's resources;

- We protect each individual's privacy and confidentiality in the use of library resources and services;

- We protect the rights of individuals to express their opinions about library resources and services;

- We celebrate and preserve our democratic society by making available the widest possible range of viewpoints, opinions, and ideas, so that all individuals have the opportunity to become lifelong learners—informed, literate, educated, and culturally enriched.

Change is constant, but these principles transcend change and endure in a dynamic technological, social, and political environment.

By embracing these principles, libraries in the United States can contribute to a future that values and protects freedom of speech in a world that celebrates both our similarities and our differences, respects individuals and their beliefs, and holds all persons truly equal and free.

Adopted February 3, 1999, by the Council of the American Library Association.

B.2. Library Bill of Rights

The American Library Association affirms that all libraries are forums for information and ideas, and that the following basic policies should guide their services.

   I. Books and other library resources should be provided for the interest, information, and enlightenment of all people of the community the library serves. Materials should not be excluded because of the origin, background, or views of those contributing to their creation.

   II. Libraries should provide materials and information presenting all points of view on current and historical issues. Materials should not be proscribed or removed because of partisan or doctrinal disapproval.

   III. Libraries should challenge censorship in the fulfillment of their responsibility to provide information and enlightenment.

   IV. Libraries should cooperate with all persons and groups concerned with resisting abridgment of free expression and free access to ideas.

   V. A person's right to use a library should not be denied or abridged because of origin, age, background, or views.

   VI. Libraries which make exhibit spaces and meeting rooms available to the public they serve should make such facilities available on an equitable basis, regardless of the beliefs or affiliations of individuals or groups requesting their use.

Adopted June 18, 1948, by the ALA Council; amended February 2, 1961; amended June 28, 1967; amended January 23, 1980; inclusion of "age" reaffirmed January 24, 1996.

B.3. Freedom to Read Statement

The freedom to read is essential to our democracy. It is continuously under attack. Private groups and public authorities in various parts of the country are working to remove or limit access to reading materials, to censor content in schools, to label "controversial" views, to distribute lists of "objectionable" books or authors, and to purge libraries. These actions apparently rise from a view that our national tradition of free expression is no longer valid; that censorship and suppression are needed to counter threats to safety or national security, as well as to avoid the subversion of politics and the corruption of morals. We, as individuals devoted to reading and as librarians and publishers responsible for disseminating ideas, wish to assert the public interest in the preservation of the freedom to read.

Most attempts at suppression rest on a denial of the fundamental premise of democracy: that the ordinary individual, by exercising critical judgment, will select the good and reject the bad. We trust Americans to recognize propaganda and misinformation, and to make their own decisions about what they read and believe. We do not believe they are prepared to sacrifice their heritage of a free press in order to be "protected" against what others think may be bad for them. We believe they still favor free enterprise in ideas and expression.

These efforts at suppression are related to a larger pattern of pressures being brought against education, the press, art and images, films, broadcast media, and the Internet. The problem is not only one of actual censorship. The shadow of fear cast by these pressures leads, we suspect, to an even larger voluntary curtailment of expression by those who seek to avoid controversy or unwelcome scrutiny by government officials.

Such pressure toward conformity is perhaps natural to a time of accelerated change. And yet suppression is never more dangerous than in such a time of social tension. Freedom has given the United States the elasticity to endure strain. Freedom keeps open the path of novel and creative solutions, and enables change to come by choice. Every silencing of a heresy, every enforcement of an orthodoxy, diminishes the toughness and resilience of our society and leaves it the less able to deal with controversy and difference.

Now as always in our history, reading is among our greatest freedoms. The freedom to read and write is almost the only means for making generally available ideas or manners of expression that can initially command only a small audience. The written word is the natural medium for the new idea and the untried voice from which come the original contributions to social growth. It is essential to the extended discussion that serious thought requires, and to the accumulation of knowledge and ideas into organized collections.

We believe that free communication is essential to the preservation of a free society and a creative culture. We believe that these pressures toward conformity present the danger of limiting the range and variety of inquiry and expression on which our democracy and our culture depend. We believe that every American community must jealously guard the freedom to publish and to circulate, in order to preserve its own freedom to read. We believe that publishers and librarians have a profound responsibility to give validity to that freedom to read by making it possible for the readers to choose freely from a variety of offerings.

The freedom to read is guaranteed by the Constitution. Those with faith in free people will stand firm on these constitutional guarantees of essential rights and will exercise the responsibilities that accompany these rights.

We therefore affirm these propositions:

1. *It is in the public interest for publishers and librarians to make available the widest diversity of views and expressions, including those that are unorthodox, unpopular, or considered dangerous by the majority.*

    Creative thought is by definition new, and what is new is different. The bearer of every new thought is a rebel until that idea is refined and tested. Totalitarian systems attempt to maintain themselves in power by the ruthless suppression of any concept that challenges the established orthodoxy. The power of a democratic system to adapt to change is vastly strengthened by the freedom of its citizens to choose widely from among conflicting opinions offered freely to them. To stifle every nonconformist idea at birth would mark the end of the democratic process. Furthermore, only through the constant activity of weighing and selecting can the democratic mind attain the strength demanded by times like these. We need to know not only what we believe but why we believe it.

2. *Publishers, librarians, and booksellers do not need to endorse every idea or presentation they make available. It would conflict with the public interest for them to establish their own political, moral, or aesthetic views as a standard for determining what should be published or circulated.*

    Publishers and librarians serve the educational process by helping to make available knowledge and ideas required for the growth of the mind and the increase of learning. They do not foster education by imposing as mentors the patterns of their own thought. The people should have the freedom to read and consider a broader range of ideas than those that may be held by any single librarian or publisher or government or church. It is wrong that what one can read should be confined to what another thinks proper.

3. *It is contrary to the public interest for publishers or librarians to bar access to writings on the basis of the personal history or political affiliations of the author.*

    No art or literature can flourish if it is to be measured by the political views or private lives of its creators. No society of free people can flourish that draws up lists of writers to whom it will not listen, whatever they may have to say.

4. *There is no place in our society for efforts to coerce the taste of others, to confine adults to the reading matter deemed suitable for adolescents, or to inhibit the efforts of writers to achieve artistic expression.*

    To some, much of modern expression is shocking. But is not much of life itself shocking? We cut off literature at the source if we prevent writers from dealing with the stuff of life. Parents and teachers have a responsibility to prepare the young to meet the diversity of experiences in life to which they will be exposed, as they have a responsibility to help them learn to think critically for themselves. These are affirmative responsibilities, not to be discharged simply by preventing them from reading works for which they are not yet prepared. In these matters values differ, and values cannot be legislated; nor can machinery be devised that will suit the demands of one group without limiting the freedom of others.

5. *It is not in the public interest to force a reader to accept the prejudgment of a label characterizing any expression or its author as subversive or dangerous.*

   The ideal of labeling presupposes the existence of individuals or groups with wisdom to determine by authority what is good or bad for others. It presupposes that individuals must be directed in making up their minds about the ideas they examine. But Americans do not need others to do their thinking for them.

6. *It is the responsibility of publishers and librarians, as guardians of the people's freedom to read, to contest encroachments upon that freedom by individuals or groups seeking to impose their own standards or tastes upon the community at large; and by the government whenever it seeks to reduce or deny public access to public information.*

   It is inevitable in the give and take of the democratic process that the political, the moral, or the aesthetic concepts of an individual or group will occasionally collide with those of another individual or group. In a free society individuals are free to determine for themselves what they wish to read, and each group is free to determine what it will recommend to its freely associated members. But no group has the right to take the law into its own hands, and to impose its own concept of politics or morality upon other members of a democratic society. Freedom is not freedom if it is accorded only to the accepted and the inoffensive. Further, democratic societies are more safe, free, and creative when the free flow of public information is not restricted by governmental prerogative or self-censorship.

7. *It is the responsibility of publishers and librarians to give full meaning to the freedom to read by providing books that enrich the quality and diversity of thought and expression. By the exercise of this affirmative responsibility, they can demonstrate that the answer to a "bad" book is a good one, the answer to a "bad" idea is a good one.*

   The freedom to read is of little consequence when the reader cannot obtain matter fit for that reader's purpose. What is needed is not only the absence of restraint, but the positive provision of opportunity for the people to read the best that has been thought and said. Books are the major channel by which the intellectual inheritance is handed down, and the principal means of its testing and growth. The defense of the freedom to read requires of all publishers and librarians the utmost of their faculties, and deserves of all Americans the fullest of their support.

We state these propositions neither lightly nor as easy generalizations. We here stake out a lofty claim for the value of the written word. We do so because we believe that it is possessed of enormous variety and usefulness, worthy of cherishing and keeping free. We realize that the application of these propositions may mean the dissemination of ideas and manners of expression that are repugnant to many persons. We do not state these propositions in the comfortable belief that what people read is unimportant. We believe rather that what people read is deeply important; that ideas can be dangerous; but that the suppression of ideas is fatal to a democratic society. Freedom itself is a dangerous way of life, but it is ours.

This statement was originally issued in May of 1953 by the Westchester Conference of the American Library Association and the American Book Publishers Council, which in 1970 consolidated with the American Educational Publishers Institute to become the Association of American Publishers.

Adopted June 25, 1953, by the ALA Council and the AAP Freedom to Read Committee; amended January 28, 1972; January 16, 1991; July 12, 2000; June 30, 2004.

A Joint Statement by:
American Library Association
Association of American Publishers

Subsequently endorsed by:
American Booksellers Foundation for Free Expression
The Association of American University Presses, Inc.
The Children's Book Council
Freedom to Read Foundation
National Association of College Stores
National Coalition Against Censorship
National Council of Teachers of English
The Thomas Jefferson Center for the Protection of Free Expression

B.4. Freedom to View Statement

The **FREEDOM TO VIEW**, along with the freedom to speak, to hear, and to read, is protected by the First Amendment to the Constitution of the United States. In a free society, there is no place for censorship of any medium of expression. Therefore these principles are affirmed:

1. To provide the broadest access to film, video, and other audiovisual materials because they are a means for the communication of ideas. Liberty of circulation is essential to insure the constitutional guarantee of freedom of expression.

2. To protect the confidentiality of all individuals and institutions using film, video, and other audiovisual materials.

3. To provide film, video, and other audiovisual materials which represent a diversity of views and expression. Selection of a work does not constitute or imply agreement with or approval of the content.

4. To provide a diversity of viewpoints without the constraint of labeling or prejudging film, video, or other audiovisual materials on the basis of the moral, religious, or political beliefs of the producer or filmmaker or on the basis of controversial content.

5. To contest vigorously, by all lawful means, every encroachment upon the public's freedom to view.

This statement was originally drafted by the Freedom to View Committee of the American Film and Video Association (formerly the Educational Film Library Association) and was adopted by the AFVA Board of Directors in February 1979. This statement was updated and approved by the AFVA Board of Directors in 1989.

Endorsed January 10, 1990, by the ALA Council.

B.5. Labeling and Rating Systems: An Interpretation of the Library Bill of Rights

Libraries do not advocate the ideas found in their collections or in resources accessible through the library. The presence of books and other resources in a library does not indicate endorsement of their contents by the library. Likewise, providing access to digital information does not indicate endorsement or approval of that information by the library. Labeling and rating systems present distinct challenges to these intellectual freedom principles.

Labels on library materials may be viewpoint-neutral directional aids designed to save the time of users, or they may be attempts to prejudice or discourage users or restrict their access to materials. When labeling is an attempt to prejudice attitudes, it is a censor's tool. The American Library Association opposes labeling as a means of predisposing people's attitudes toward library materials.

Prejudicial labels are designed to restrict access, based on a value judgment that the content, language, or themes of the material, or the background or views of the creator(s) of the material, render it inappropriate or offensive for all or certain groups of users. The prejudicial label is used to warn, discourage, or prohibit users or certain groups of users from accessing the material. Such labels sometimes are used to place materials in restricted locations where access depends on staff intervention.

Viewpoint-neutral directional aids facilitate access by making it easier for users to locate materials. The materials are housed on open shelves and are equally accessible to all users, who may choose to consult or ignore the directional aids at their own discretion.

Directional aids can have the effect of prejudicial labels when their implementation becomes proscriptive rather than descriptive. When directional aids are used to forbid access or to suggest moral or doctrinal endorsement, the effect is the same as prejudicial labeling.

Many organizations use rating systems as a means of advising either their members or the general public regarding the organizations' opinions of the contents and suitability or appropriate age for use of certain books, films, recordings, Web sites, games, or other materials. The adoption, enforcement, or endorsement of any of these rating systems by a library violates the Library Bill of Rights. When requested, librarians should provide information about rating systems equitably, regardless of viewpoint.

Adopting such systems into law or library policy may be unconstitutional. If labeling or rating systems are mandated by law, the library should seek legal advice regarding the law's applicability to library operations.

Libraries sometimes acquire resources that include ratings as part of their packaging. Librarians should not endorse the inclusion of such rating systems; however, removing or destroying the ratings—if placed there by, or with permission of, the copyright holder—could constitute expurgation. In addition, the inclusion of ratings on bibliographic records in library catalogs is a violation of the Library Bill of Rights.

Prejudicial labeling and ratings presuppose the existence of individuals or groups with wisdom to determine by authority what is appropriate or inappropriate for others. They presuppose that individuals must be directed in making up their minds about the ideas they examine. The American Library Association affirms the rights of individuals to form their own opinions about resources they choose to read or view.

Adopted July 13, 1951, by the ALA Council; amended June 25, 1971; July 1, 1981; June 26, 1990; January 19, 2005; July 15, 2009.

B.6. Access to Digital Information, Services, and Networks: An Interpretation of the Library Bill of Rights

Introduction

Freedom of expression is an inalienable human right and the foundation for self-government. Freedom of expression encompasses the freedom of speech and the corollary right to receive information.[1] Libraries and librarians protect and promote these rights regardless of the format or technology employed to create and disseminate information.

The American Library Association expresses the fundamental principles of librarianship in its Code of Ethics as well as in the Library Bill of Rights and its Interpretations. These principles guide librarians and library governing bodies in addressing issues of intellectual freedom that arise when the library provides access to digital information, services, and networks.

Libraries empower users by offering opportunities both for accessing the broadest range of information created by others and for creating and sharing information. Digital resources enhance the ability of libraries to fulfill this responsibility.

Libraries should regularly review issues arising from digital creation, distribution, retrieval, and archiving of information in the context of constitutional principles and ALA policies so that fundamental and traditional tenets of librarianship are upheld. Although digital information flows across boundaries and barriers despite attempts by individuals, governments, and private entities to channel or control it, many people lack access or capability to use or create digital information effectively.

In making decisions about how to offer access to digital information, services, and networks, each library should consider intellectual freedom principles in the context of its mission, goals, objectives, cooperative agreements, and the needs of the entire community it serves.

The Rights of Users

All library system and network policies, procedures, or regulations relating to digital information and services should be scrutinized for potential violations of user rights. User policies should be developed according to the policies and guidelines established by the American Library Association, including "Guidelines for the Development and Implementation of Policies, Regulations, and Procedures Affecting Access to Library Materials, Services, and Facilities."

Users' access should not be restricted or denied for expressing, receiving, creating, or participating in constitutionally protected speech. If access is restricted or denied for behavioral or other reasons, users should be provided due process, including, but not limited to, formal notice and a means of appeal.

Information retrieved, utilized, or created digitally is constitutionally protected unless determined otherwise by a court of competent jurisdiction. These rights extend to minors as well as adults ("Free Access to Libraries for Minors"; "Access to Resources and Services in the School Library Media Program"; "Access for Children and Young Adults to Nonprint Materials"; and "Minors and Internet Interactivity").[2]

Libraries should use technology to enhance, not deny, digital access. Users have the right to be free of unreasonable limitations or conditions set by libraries, librarians, system administrators, vendors, network service providers, or others. Contracts, agreements, and licenses entered into by libraries on behalf of their users should not violate this right. Libraries should provide library users the training and assistance necessary to find, evaluate, and use information effectively.

Users have both the right of confidentiality and the right of privacy. The library should uphold these rights by policy, procedure, and practice in accordance with "Privacy: An Interpretation of the Library Bill of Rights," and "Importance of Education to Intellectual Freedom: An Interpretation of the Library Bill of Rights."

Equity of Access

The digital environment provides expanding opportunities for everyone to participate in the information society, but individuals may face serious barriers to access.

Digital information, services, and networks provided directly or indirectly by the library should be equally, readily, and equitably accessible to all library users. American Library Association policies oppose the charging of user fees for the provision of information services by libraries that receive support from public funds (50.3 "Free Access to Information"; 53.1.14 "Economic Barriers to Information Access"; 60.1.1 "Minority Concerns Policy Objectives"; 61.1 "Library Services for the Poor Policy Objectives"). All libraries should develop policies concerning access to digital information that are consistent with ALA's policies and guidelines, including "Economic Barriers to Information Access: An Interpretation of the Library Bill of Rights," "Guidelines for the Development and Implementation of Policies, Regulations and Procedures Affecting Access to Library Materials, Services and Facilities," and "Services to Persons with Disabilities: An Interpretation of the Library Bill of Rights."

Information Resources and Access

Libraries, acting within their mission and objectives, must support access to information on all subjects that serve the needs or interests of each user, regardless of the user's age or the content of the material. In order to preserve the cultural record and to prevent the loss of information, libraries may need to expand their selection or collection development policies to ensure preservation, in appropriate formats, of information obtained digitally. Libraries have an obligation to provide access to government information available in digital format.

Providing connections to global information, services, and networks is not the same as selecting and purchasing materials for a library collection. Libraries and librarians should not deny or limit access to digital information because of its allegedly controversial content or because of a librarian's personal beliefs or fear of confrontation. Furthermore, libraries and librarians should not deny access to digital information solely on the grounds that it is perceived to lack value. Parents and legal guardians who are concerned about their children's use of digital resources should provide guidance to their own children. Some information accessed digitally may not meet a library's selection or collection development policy. It is, therefore, left to each user to determine what is appropriate.

Publicly funded libraries have a legal obligation to provide access to constitutionally protected information. Federal, state, county, municipal, local, or library governing bodies sometimes require the use of Internet filters or other technological measures that block access to constitutionally protected information, contrary to the Library Bill of Rights (ALA Policy Manual, 53.1.17, Resolution on the Use of Filtering Software in Libraries). If a library uses a technological measure that blocks access to information, it should be set at the least restrictive level in order to minimize the blocking of constitutionally protected speech. Adults retain the right to access all constitutionally protected information and to ask for the technological measure to be disabled in a timely manner. Minors also retain the right to access constitutionally protected information and, at the minimum, have the right to ask the library or librarian to provide access to erroneously blocked information in a timely manner. Libraries and librarians have an obligation to inform users of these rights and to provide the means to exercise these rights.[3]

Digital resources provide unprecedented opportunities to expand the scope of information available to users. Libraries and librarians should provide access to information presenting all points of view. The provision of access does not imply sponsorship or endorsement. These principles pertain to digital resources as much as they do to the more traditional sources of information in libraries ("Diversity in Collection Development").

1. *Martin v. Struthers*, 319 U.S. 141 (1943); *Lamont v. Postmaster General*, 381 U.S. 301 (1965); Susan Nevelow Mart, "The Right to Receive Information," 95 *Law Library Journal* 2 (2003).

2. *Tinker v. Des Moines Independent Community School District*, 393 U.S. 503 (1969); *Board of Education, Island Trees Union Free School District No. 26 v. Pico*, 457 U.S. 853 (1982); *American Amusement Machine Association v. Teri Kendrick*, 244 F.3d 954 (7th Cir. 2001); cert. denied, 534 U.S. 994 (2001).

3. "If some libraries do not have the capacity to unblock specific Web sites or to disable the filter or if it is shown that an adult user's election to view constitutionally protected Internet material is burdened in some other substantial way, that would be the subject for an as-applied challenge, not the facial challenge made in this case." *United States, et al. v. American Library Association*, 539 U.S. 194 (2003) (Justice Kennedy, concurring).

See also: "Questions and Answers on Access to Digital Information, Services and Networks: An Interpretation of the Library Bill of Rights."

Adopted January 24, 1996; amended January 19, 2005; and July 15, 2009, by the ALA Council.

B.7. Free Access to Libraries for Minors: An Interpretation of the Library Bill of Rights

Library policies and procedures that effectively deny minors equal and equitable access to all library resources and services available to other users violate the Library Bill of Rights. The American Library Association opposes all attempts to restrict access to library services, materials, and facilities based on the age of library users.

Article V of the Library Bill of Rights states, "A person's right to use a library should not be denied or abridged because of origin, age, background, or views." The "right to use a library" includes free access to, and unrestricted use of, all the services, materials, and facilities the library has to offer. Every restriction on access to, and use of, library resources, based solely on the chronological age, educational level, literacy skills, or legal emancipation of users violates Article V.

Libraries are charged with the mission of providing services and developing resources to meet the diverse information needs and interests of the communities they serve. Services, materials, and facilities that fulfill the needs and interests of library users at different stages in their personal development are a necessary part of library resources. The needs and interests of each library user, and resources appropriate to meet those needs and interests, must be determined on an individual basis. Librarians cannot predict what resources will best fulfill the needs and interests of any individual user based on a single criterion such as chronological age, educational level, literacy skills, or legal emancipation. Equitable access to all library resources and services shall not be abridged through restrictive scheduling or use policies.

Libraries should not limit the selection and development of library resources simply because minors will have access to them. Institutional self-censorship diminishes the credibility of the library in the community, and restricts access for all library users.

Children and young adults unquestionably possess First Amendment rights, including the right to receive information through the library in print, nonprint, or digital format. Constitutionally protected speech cannot be suppressed solely to protect children or young adults from ideas or images a legislative body believes to be unsuitable for them.[1] Librarians and library governing bodies should not resort to age restrictions in an effort to avoid actual or anticipated objections, because only a court of law can determine whether material is not constitutionally protected.

The mission, goals, and objectives of libraries cannot authorize librarians or library governing bodies to assume, abrogate, or overrule the rights and responsibilities of parents and guardians. As "Libraries: An American Value" states, "We affirm the responsibility and the right of all parents and guardians to guide their own children's use of the library and its resources and services." Librarians and library governing bodies cannot assume the role of parents or the functions of parental authority in the private relationship between parent and child. Librarians and governing bodies should maintain that only parents and guardians have the right and the responsibility to determine their children's—and only their children's—access to library resources. Parents and guardians who do not want their children to have access to specific library services, materials, or facilities should so advise their children.

Lack of access to information can be harmful to minors. Librarians and library governing bodies have a public and professional obligation to ensure that all members of the community they serve have free, equal, and equitable access to the entire range of library resources regardless of content, approach, format, or amount of detail. This principle of library service applies equally to all users, minors as well as adults. Librarians and library governing bodies must uphold this principle in order to provide adequate and effective service to minors.

1. See *Erznoznik v. City of Jacksonville*, 422 U.S. 205 (1975): "Speech that is neither obscene as to youths nor subject to some other legitimate proscription cannot be suppressed solely to protect the young from ideas or images that a legislative body thinks unsuitable for them. In most circumstances, the values protected by the First Amendment are no less applicable when government seeks to control the flow of information to minors." See also *Tinker v. Des Moines School Dist.*, 393 U.S. 503 (1969); *West Virginia Bd. of Ed. v. Barnette*, 319 U.S. 624 (1943); *AAMA v. Kendrick*, 244 F.3d 572 (7th Cir. 2001).

See also: "Access to Resources and Services in the School Library Media Program" and "Access for Children and Young Adults to Nonprint Materials."

Adopted June 30, 1972, by the ALA Council; amended July 1, 1981; July 3, 1991; June 30, 2004; July 2, 2008.

B.8. Meeting Rooms: An Interpretation of the Library Bill of Rights

Many libraries provide meeting rooms for individuals and groups as part of a program of service. Article VI of the Library Bill of Rights states that such facilities should be made available to the public served by the given library "on an equitable basis, regardless of the beliefs or affiliations of individuals or groups requesting their use."

Libraries maintaining meeting room facilities should develop and publish policy statements governing use. These statements can properly define time, place, or manner of use; such qualifications should not pertain to the content of a meeting or to the beliefs or affiliations of the sponsors. These statements should be made available in any commonly used language within the community served.

If meeting rooms in libraries supported by public funds are made available to the general public for non-library-sponsored events, the library may not exclude any group based on the subject matter to be discussed or based on the ideas that the group advocates. For example, if a library allows charities and sports clubs to discuss their activities in library meeting rooms, then the library should not exclude partisan political or religious groups from discussing their activities in the same facilities. If a library opens its meeting rooms to a wide variety of civic organizations, then the library may not deny access to a religious organization. Libraries may wish to post a permanent notice near the meeting room stating that the library does not advocate or endorse the viewpoints of meetings or meeting room users.

Written policies for meeting room use should be stated in inclusive rather than exclusive terms. For example, a policy that the library's facilities are open "to organizations engaged in educational, cultural, intellectual, or charitable activities" is an inclusive statement of the limited uses to which the facilities may be put. This defined limitation would permit religious groups to use the facilities because they engage in intellectual activities, but would exclude most commercial uses of the facility.

A publicly supported library may limit use of its meeting rooms to strictly "library-related" activities, provided that the limitation is clearly circumscribed and is viewpoint neutral.

Written policies may include limitations on frequency of use, and whether or not meetings held in library meeting rooms must be open to the public. If state and local laws permit private as well as public sessions of meetings in libraries, libraries may choose to offer both options. The same standard should be applicable to all.

If meetings are open to the public, libraries should include in their meeting room policy statement a section that addresses admission fees. If admission fees are permitted, libraries shall seek to make it possible that these fees do not limit access to individuals who may be unable to pay, but who wish to attend the meeting. Article V of the Library Bill of Rights states that "a person's right to use a library should not be denied or abridged because of origin, age, background, or views." It is inconsistent with Article V to restrict indirectly access to library meeting rooms based on an individual's or group's ability to pay for that access.

Adopted July 2, 1991, by the ALA Council.

B.9. Minors and Internet Interactivity: An Interpretation of the Library Bill of Rights

The digital environment offers opportunities for accessing, creating, and sharing information. The rights of minors to retrieve, interact with, and create information posted on the Internet in schools and libraries are extensions of their First Amendment rights. (See also other interpretations of the Library Bill of Rights, including "Access to Digital Information, Services, and Networks," "Free Access to Libraries for Minors," and "Access for Children and Young Adults to Nonprint Materials.")

Academic pursuits of minors can be strengthened with the use of interactive Web tools, allowing young people to create documents and share them online; upload pictures, videos, and graphic material; revise public documents; and add tags to online content to classify and organize information. Instances of inappropriate use of such academic tools should be addressed as individual behavior issues, not as justification for restricting or banning access to interactive technology. Schools and libraries should ensure that institutional environments offer opportunities for students to use interactive Web tools constructively in their academic pursuits, as the benefits of shared learning are well documented.

Personal interactions of minors can be enhanced by social tools available through the Internet. Social networking Web sites allow the creation of online communities that feature an open exchange of information in various forms, such as images, videos, blog posts, and discussions about common interests. Interactive Web tools help children and young adults learn about and organize social, civic, and extracurricular activities. Many interactive sites invite users to establish online identities, share personal information, create Web content, and join social networks. Parents and guardians play a critical role in preparing their children for participation in online activity by communicating their personal family values and by monitoring their children's use of the Internet. Parents and guardians are responsible for what their children—and only their children—access on the Internet in libraries.

The use of interactive Web tools poses two competing intellectual freedom issues—the protection of minors' privacy and the right of free speech. Some have expressed concerns regarding what they perceive is an increased vulnerability of young people in the online environment when they use interactive sites to post personally identifiable information. In an effort to protect minors' privacy, adults sometimes restrict access to interactive Web environments. Filters, for example, are sometimes used to restrict access by youth to interactive social networking tools, but at the same time deny minors' rights to free expression on the Internet. Prohibiting children and young adults from using social networking sites does not teach safe behavior and leaves youth without the necessary knowledge and skills to protect their privacy or engage in responsible speech. Instead of restricting or denying access to the Internet, librarians and teachers should educate minors to participate responsibly, ethically, and safely.

The First Amendment applies to speech created by minors on interactive sites. Usage of these social networking sites in a school or library allows minors to access and create resources that fulfill their interests and needs for information, for social connection with peers, and for participation in a community of learners. Restricting expression and access to interactive Web sites because the sites provide tools for sharing information with others violates the tenets of the Library Bill of Rights. It is the responsibility of librarians and educators to monitor threats to the intellectual freedom of minors and to advocate for extending access to interactive applications on the Internet. As defenders of intellectual freedom and the First Amendment, libraries and librarians have a responsibility to offer unrestricted access to Internet interactivity in accordance with local, state, and federal laws and to advocate for greater access where it is abridged. School and library professionals should work closely with young people to help them learn skills and attitudes that will prepare them to be responsible, effective, and productive communicators in a free society.

Adopted July 15, 2009, by the ALA Council.

B.10. Restricted Access to Library Materials: An Interpretation of the Library Bill of Rights

Libraries are a traditional forum for the open exchange of information. Restricting access to library materials violates the basic tenets of the Library Bill of Rights.

Some libraries block access to certain materials by placing physical or virtual barriers between the user and those materials. For example, materials are sometimes placed in a "locked case," "adults only," "restricted shelf," or "high-demand" collection. Access to certain materials is sometimes restricted to protect them from theft or mutilation, or because of statutory authority or institutional mandate.

In some libraries, access is restricted based on computerized reading management programs that assign reading levels to books and/or users and limit choice to those materials on the program's reading list. Materials that are not on the reading management list have been removed from the collection in some school libraries. Organizing collections by reading management program level, ability, grade, or age level is another example of restricted access. Even though the chronological age or grade level of users is not representative of their information needs or total reading abilities, users may feel inhibited from selecting resources located in areas that do not correspond to their assigned characteristics.

Physical and virtual restrictions on access to library materials may generate psychological, service, or language skills barriers to access as well. Because restricted materials often deal with controversial, unusual, or sensitive subjects, having to ask a librarian or circulation clerk for access to them may be embarrassing or inhibiting for patrons desiring the materials. Even when a title is listed in the catalog with a reference to its restricted status, a barrier is placed between the patron and the publication (see also "Labels and Rating Systems"). Because restricted materials often feature information that some people consider objectionable, potential library users may be predisposed to think of the materials as objectionable and, therefore, be reluctant to ask for access to them.

Although federal and state statutes require libraries that accept specific types of state and/or federal funding to install filters that limit access to Internet resources for minors and adults, filtering software applied to Internet stations in some libraries may prevent users from finding targeted categories of information, much of which is constitutionally protected. The use of Internet filters must be addressed through library policies and procedures to ensure that users receive information and that filters do not prevent users from exercising their First Amendment rights. Users have the right to unfiltered access to constitutionally protected information (see also "Access to Electronic Information, Services, and Resources").

Library policies that restrict access to materials for any reason must be carefully formulated and administered to ensure they do not violate established principles of intellectual freedom. This caution is reflected in ALA policies, such as "Evaluating Library Collections," "Free Access to Libraries for Minors," "Preservation Policy," and the ACRL "Code of Ethics for Special Collections Librarians."

Donated materials require special consideration. In keeping with the "Joint Statement on Access" of the American Library Association and Society of American Archivists, libraries should avoid accepting donor agreements or entering into contracts that impose permanent restrictions on special collections. As stated in the "Joint Statement on Access," it is the responsibility of a library with such collections "to make available original research materials in its possession on equal terms of access."

A primary goal of the library profession is to facilitate access to all points of view on current and historical issues. All proposals for restricted access should be carefully scrutinized to ensure that the purpose is not to suppress a viewpoint or to place a barrier between users and content. Libraries must maintain policies and procedures that serve the diverse needs of their users and protect the First Amendment right to receive information.

Adopted February 2, 1973, by the ALA Council; amended July 1, 1981; July 3, 1991; July 12, 2000; June 30, 2004; January 28, 2009.

B.11. The Universal Right to Free Expression: An Interpretation of the Library Bill of Rights

Freedom of expression is an inalienable human right and the foundation for self-government. Freedom of expression encompasses the freedoms of speech, press, religion, assembly, and association, and the corollary right to receive information.

The American Library Association endorses this principle, which is also set forth in the Universal Declaration of Human Rights, adopted by the United Nations General Assembly. The Preamble of this document states that "...recognition of the inherent dignity and of the equal and inalienable rights of all members of the human family is the foundation of freedom, justice, and peace in the world..." and "...the advent of a world in which human beings shall enjoy freedom of speech and belief and freedom from fear and want has been proclaimed as the highest aspiration of the common people...."

Article 18 of this document states:

> Everyone has the right to freedom of thought, conscience and religion; this right includes freedom to change his religion or belief, and freedom, either alone or in community with others and in public or private, to manifest his religion or belief in teaching, practice, worship and observance.

Article 19 states:

> Everyone has the right to freedom of opinion and expression; this right includes freedom to hold opinions without interference and to seek, receive and impart information and ideas through any media regardless of frontiers.

Article 20 states:

1. Everyone has the right to freedom of peaceful assembly and association.
2. No one may be compelled to belong to an association.

We affirm our belief that these are inalienable rights of every person, regardless of origin, age, background, or views. We embody our professional commitment to these principles in the Library Bill of Rights and Code of Ethics, as adopted by the American Library Association.

We maintain that these are universal principles and should be applied by libraries and librarians throughout the world. The American Library Association's policy on International Relations reflects these objectives:

> to encourage the exchange, dissemination, and access to information and the unrestricted flow of library materials in all formats throughout the world.

We know that censorship, ignorance, and limitations on the free flow of information are the tools of tyranny and oppression. We believe that ideas and information topple the walls of hate and fear and build bridges of cooperation and understanding far more effectively than weapons and armies.

The American Library Association is unswerving in its commitment to human rights and intellectual freedom; the two are inseparably linked and inextricably entwined. Freedom of opinion and expression is not derived from or dependent on any form of government or political power. This right is inherent in every individual. It cannot be surrendered, nor can it be denied. True justice comes from the exercise of this right.

We recognize the power of information and ideas to inspire justice, to restore freedom and dignity to the oppressed, and to change the hearts and minds of the oppressors.

Courageous men and women, in difficult and dangerous circumstances throughout human history, have demonstrated that freedom lives in the human heart and cries out for justice even in the face of threats, enslavement, imprisonment, torture, exile, and death. We draw inspiration from their example. They challenge us to remain steadfast in our most basic professional responsibility to promote and defend the right of free expression.

There is no good censorship. Any effort to restrict free expression and the free flow of information aids the oppressor. Fighting oppression with censorship is self-defeating.

Threats to the freedom of expression of any person anywhere are threats to the freedom of all people everywhere. Violations of human rights and the right of free expression have been recorded in virtually every country and society across the globe.

In response to these violations, we affirm these principles:

- The American Library Association opposes any use of governmental prerogative that leads to the intimidation of individuals that prevents them from exercising their rights to hold opinions without interference, and to seek, receive, and impart information and ideas. We urge libraries and librarians everywhere to resist such abuse of governmental power, and to support those against whom such governmental power has been employed.

- The American Library Association condemns any governmental effort to involve libraries and librarians in restrictions on the right of any individual to hold opinions without interference, and to seek, receive, and impart information and ideas. Such restrictions pervert the function of the library and violate the professional responsibilities of librarians.

- The American Library Association rejects censorship in any form. Any action that denies the inalienable human rights of individuals only damages the will to resist oppression, strengthens the hand of the oppressor, and undermines the cause of justice.

- The American Library Association will not abrogate these principles. We believe that censorship corrupts the cause of justice, and contributes to the demise of freedom.

Adopted January 16, 1991, by the ALA Council.

B.12. Statement on Library Use of Filtering Software

American Library Association Intellectual Freedom Committee

On June 26, 1997, the United States Supreme Court in *Reno, Attorney General of the United States, et al. v. American Civil Liberties Union*, et al., issued a sweeping reaffirmation of core First Amendment principles and held that communications over the Internet deserve the highest level of constitutional protection.

The Court's most fundamental holding was that communications on the Internet deserve the same level of constitutional protection as books, magazines, newspapers, and speakers on a street corner soapbox. The Court found that the Internet "constitutes a vast platform from which to address and hear from a world-wide audience of millions of readers, viewers, researchers, and buyers," and that "any person with a phone line can become a town crier with a voice that resonates farther than it could from any soapbox."

For libraries, the most critical holding of the Supreme Court is that libraries that make content available on the Internet can continue to do so with the same constitutional protections that apply to the books on libraries' shelves. The Court's conclusion that "the vast democratic fora of the Internet" merit full constitutional protection serves to protect libraries that provide their patrons with access to the Internet. The Court recognized the importance of enabling individuals to receive speech from the entire world and to speak to the entire world.

Libraries provide those opportunities to many who would not otherwise have them. The Supreme Court's decision protects that access.

The use in libraries of software filters to block constitutionally protected speech is inconsistent with the United States Constitution and federal law and may lead to legal exposure for the library and its governing authorities. The American Library Association affirms that the use of filtering software by libraries to block access to constitutionally protected speech violates the Library Bill of Rights.

What Is Blocking/Filtering Software?

Blocking/filtering software is a mechanism used to:

- restrict access to Internet content, based on an internal database of the product, or;
- restrict access to Internet content through a database maintained external to the product itself, or;
- restrict access to Internet content to certain ratings assigned to those sites by a third party, or;
- restrict access to Internet content by scanning text, based on a keyword or phrase or text string, or;
- restrict access to Internet content by scanning pixels, based on color or tone, or;
- restrict access to Internet content based on the source of the information.

Problems with the Use of Blocking/Filtering Software in Libraries

- Publicly supported libraries are governmental institutions subject to the First Amendment, which forbids them from restricting information based on viewpoint or content discrimination.
- Libraries are places of inclusion rather than exclusion. Current blocking/ filtering software not only prevents access to what some may consider "objectionable" material, but also blocks information protected by the First Amendment. The result is that legal and useful material will inevitably be blocked.
- Filters can impose the producer's viewpoint on the community.
- Producers do not generally reveal what is being blocked, or provide methods for users to reach sites that were inadvertently blocked.
- Criteria used to block content are vaguely defined and subjectively applied.
- The vast majority of Internet sites are informative and useful. Blocking/ filtering software often blocks access to materials it is not designed to block.

- Most blocking/filtering software was designed for the home market and was intended to respond to the preferences of parents making decisions for their children. As these products have moved into the library market, they have created a dissonance with the basic mission of libraries. Libraries are responsible for serving a broad and diverse community with different preferences and views. Blocking Internet sites is antithetical to library missions because it requires the library to limit information access.

- Filtering all Internet access is a one-size-fits-all "solution," which cannot adapt to the varying ages and maturity levels of individual users.

- A role of librarians is to advise and assist users in selecting information resources. Parents and only parents have the right and responsibility to restrict their own children's access—and only their own children's access—to library resources, including the Internet. Librarians do not serve in loco parentis.

- Library use of blocking/filtering software creates an implied contract with parents that their children will not be able to access material on the Internet that they do not wish their children to read or view. Libraries will be unable to fulfill this implied contract, due to the technological limitations of the software.

- Laws prohibiting the production or distribution of child pornography and obscenity apply to the Internet. These laws provide protection for libraries and their users.

What Can Your Library Do to Promote Access to the Internet?

- Educate yourself, your staff, library board, governing bodies, community leaders, parents, elected officials, etc., about the Internet and how best to take advantage of the wealth of information available. Information on libraries and the Internet is available on the OIF Web site at Filters and Filtering.

- Uphold the First Amendment by establishing and implementing written guidelines and policies on Internet use in your library in keeping with your library's overall policies on access to library materials. Information on Internet Use Policies is available on the OIF Web site at Checklist for Creating an Internet Use Policy. (See also "Internet Filtering Statements of State Library Associations" at Resolutions of State Library Associations Supporting Legal Action by the American Library Association to Challenge CIPA in Federal Courts and "Access to Electronic Information, Services, and Networks: An Interpretation of the Library Bill of Rights" at Access to Electronic Information, Services, and Networks.)

- Promote Internet use by facilitating user access to Web sites that satisfy user interest and needs.

- Create and promote library Web pages designed both for general use and for use by children. These pages should point to sites that have been reviewed by library staff.

- Consider using privacy screens or arranging terminals away from public view to protect a user's confidentiality.
- Provide Internet information and training for parents and children on Internet use which will include the wide variety of useful resources on the Internet, child safety on the Internet, limitations of filtering software, and library rules regarding time, place, and manner restriction.
- Establish and implement user behavior policies.

ALA Intellectual Freedom Committee
July 1, 1997; Rev. November 17, 2000

For further information on this topic, contact the ALA Office for Intellectual Freedom at 800/545-2433, ext. 4223, by fax at (312) 280-2447, or by e-mail at oif@ala.org.

B.13. ALA Resolution on the Reauthorization of the USA PATRIOT Act

Resolution on the Reauthorization of Section 215 of the USA PATRIOT Act

WHEREAS, freedom of thought is the most basic of all freedoms and is inextricably linked to the free and open exchange of knowledge and information; and these freedoms can be preserved only in a society in which privacy rights are rigorously protected; and

WHEREAS, the American Library Association (ALA) is committed to preserving the free and open exchange of knowledge and information and the privacy rights of all—library users, library employees, and the general public; and

WHEREAS, ALA opposes any use of governmental power to suppress the free and open exchange of knowledge and information; and

WHEREAS, the USA PATRIOT Act includes provisions such as Section 215 that threaten the free and open exchange of knowledge and information; and

WHEREAS, three sections of the USA PATRIOT Act, including Section 215, are scheduled to sunset on December 31, 2009; and

WHEREAS, Section 215 of the USA PATRIOT Act allows the government to request and obtain library records secretly for large numbers of individuals without any reason to believe they are involved in illegal activity; and

WHEREAS, orders issued under Section 215 automatically impose a nondisclosure or gag order on the recipients, thereby prohibiting the reporting of abuse of government authority and abrogating the recipients' First Amendment rights; and

WHEREAS, the Foreign Intelligence Surveillance Act (FISA) Court has issued more than 220 Section 215 orders between 2005 and 2007, some of which may have been issued to libraries; and

WHEREAS, the Department of Justice Office of the Inspector General reported that the "FISA Court twice refused Section 215 orders based on concerns that the investigation was premised on protected First Amendment activity"; now, therefore be it

RESOLVED:

1) that the American Library Association urges Congress to allow section 215 of the USA PATRIOT Act to sunset.

2) that the American Library Association communicate this resolution to the U.S. Congress, the President of the United States and others as appropriate.

B.14. ALTAFF Statement on Legal Limits of Lobbying for Nonprofits

Advocacy Campaigns: Legal Limits on Spending for Nonprofits

Libraries across the country are benefiting by their outspoken Friends groups. Friends have waged successful campaigns to pass bond issues and referendums and have used the power of their voices to ensure that the library's budget isn't reduced or that it is increased sufficiently to enable it to meet the needs of the community.

The following information is based on IRS rules for nonprofit 501(c)(3) organizations engaging in lobbying and advocacy and ALTAFF's interpretation of those rules. Is it really okay for Friends groups as nonprofit organizations to lobby or advocate on behalf of their library? Happily, the answer is "Yes!"

The IRS recognizes two different kinds of "advocacy." The first is called lobbying and it is when the Friends group itself or its members work to influence policy or legislation in favor of the library. Generally speaking, a Friends group can spend up to 20 percent of its yearly expenditures on these activities if their annual expenditures do not exceed $500,000. The formula changes for groups spending more and you can find out more about these formulas in ALTAFF's Friends and Foundations Zone or at the IRS Web site, www.irs.gov (see Chapter 3 of Publication 557).

The other type of "advocacy" the IRS calls grassroots lobbying and this is when a Friends group (or other nonprofit) works to get the general public to take a specific action on behalf of the library such as asking the public to "vote yes," or "call the mayor." In this case, the group can spend 25 percent of the 20 percent allotted above.

For example, if your group spends $20,000 a year in support of the library, $4,000 can be spent for lobbying (20 percent) and $1,000 can be spent on grassroots lobbying.

Remember, however, that it doesn't have to cost a lot of money to wage a successful advocacy campaign. So much of what Friends do in an advocacy campaign is educating the public about what is at stake . . . and there is no legal limit on spending money to inform or educate. Also, by using your newsletter, writing letters to the editor, or lobbying on your Web site, you are not spending much money at all!

So . . . are there any political activities that are strictly forbidden? Again, the answer is yes. Friends groups (or any 501(c)(3) organization) may not advocate, lobby, or engage in grassroots lobbying on behalf of any candidate for office. Other than this restriction, however, the IRS does allow for some activity for nonprofits to engage in advocacy.

The Friends and Foundations Zone on the ALTAFF Web site has more information on Friends and advocacy along with samples about how Friends can advocate for their libraries on a small budget.

Association of Library Trustees, Advocates, Friends and Foundations
Sally Gardner Reed
Executive Director
(800) 545-2433, ext. 2161
fax (215) 545-3821
109 S. 13th St., Suite 3N
Philadelphia, PA 19107
www.ala.org/altaff

Index

About the Authors
and ALTAFF

Sally Gardner Reed is the executive director of the Association of Library Trustees, Advocates, Friends and Foundations (ALTAFF), a division of the American Library Association. She is the author of eight books on library management, advocacy, volunteers, and fund-raising, and numerous articles for professional library journals. She has presented programs and workshops to hundreds of Friends of Library groups, library boards, and librarian groups nationally and internationally. Reed is the 2000 recipient of ALA's Herbert and Virginia White Award for promoting libraries and librarianship.

Jillian Kalonick is the marketing/public relations specialist for the Association of Library Trustees, Advocates, Friends and Foundations (ALTAFF), a division of the American Library Association. Jillian has worked for public libraries since 1994, most recently at Princeton (NJ) Public Library and Easttown (PA) Library & Information Center. She has also worked as a journalist and editor. She earned a master's degree in library and information science from Drexel University and a bachelor's degree in English from Hollins University.

ALTAFF is a division of the American Library Association (ALA) with approximately 5,000 Friends of Library, Trustee, Foundation, and individual members and affiliates representing hundreds of thousands of library supporters. Begun in early 2009 with the merger of Friends of Libraries U.S.A. (FOLUSA) and the Association for Library Trustees and Advocates (ALTA), the new division brings together Trustees and Friends into a partnership that unites the voices of citizens who support libraries to create a powerful force for libraries in the twenty-first century.